Test Prep Math

Level 2

Brian P. Murray

ISBN: 1530186234
ISBN-13: 978-1530186235

Introduction to Test Prep Math

The official goal of Test Prep Math Level 2 is to put your child in the 99th percentile of math students, to provide your child with the thinking skills and problem solving skills that your child needs to excel in all subjects, to give your child the skills to get above the 95% level of a cognitive skills test and standardized tests, and to prepare your child for advanced math that they will take 5 years later.

These are awesome goals.

To restate the objectives of this book in more concrete terms, the goal of this workbook is to describe the tools that children at the 99th percentile use to conquer math, provide material that forces the child to use these skills, and provide coaching advice to parents to teach these skills.

The workbook starts with 5 simple warm up problems, and then questions get harder and goofier. Expect both 2nd and 3rd graders to spend up to 30 minutes evaluating and solving each question. While the arithmetic is simple, the questions are challenging, and multiple attempts are expected.

Which level is more appropriate, Level 2 or Level 3? It doesn't depend on age or how far the child is ahead in arithmetic or what your child's grade is in math. Level 2 and Level 3 differ in the demands placed on working memory, attention span, tolerance for frustration, and your child's ability to read and think through complicated problems. Either book will build working memory and teach thinking skills and grit, but Level 3 can be really painful if your child is used to doing quick arithmetic problems that require nothing more than memorizing math facts.

When we first used this material, my children were offended that I was asking them to think and let me know it in a variety of ways. In school, material is thoroughly explained before the child has to do 20 or 30 easy calculation problems that require few skills. The problems in this book are the opposite. It took us a month to change the culture. The intended short term payoff, especially in working memory and logic had an immediate payoff. The longer term payoff is way beyond my expectations.

Two Problem Types

There are two sections in this book. The first section contains word problems. These word problems on their own are designed to teach all of the skills required for success in math and to some extent, other subjects.   Making adequate progress on the first section is required to tackle the second section.

I created the second section for two reasons. First, I want a practice book of quantitative questions that is way beyond the difficulty level of test questions that could appear on a cognitive abilities test.   Test prep workbooks suffer from being way too easy. Secondly, the easy arithmetic material in early grades is followed by much more difficult material in later grades culminating in abstract thinking. A bright child staking through arithmetic in grades 1 through 4 is not going to exercise any skills, and 4 years later the result may be a train wreck. I developed Section 2 as way to avoid the 4th grade train wreck.

It may take a month to get past the first problem in Section 2, and each problem thereafter might take 20 minutes, but the outcome is worth it.

Each problem, especially at the end Section 2, might take a child 30 minutes, and I recommend one a day.

The best way to do this workbook is a word problem a day, maybe 4 times a week. At some point, the child may do an extra problem from Section 2 or a few problems from Section 2 instead of a word problem. After a few months, both parent and child should have a brand new approach to academic work and your child can do the rest of the book more quickly.

I will get asked this question from some parents: "How did you get your child to do these problems? We can't get past the first question." The answer is that we concentrated on building skills with Section 1, and tried the first question from Section 2 every other week until it was doable. When Section 2 problems got ridiculously hard, we went slower and did less of them each week.

To help you better understand Section 2, let me provide a basketball analogy. When the team comes into the gym for practice, the coach makes them run laps around the cold gym until the team is warmed up. Next, the team might do drills where they stand in a line and take turns doing layups or passing the ball to each other. School curriculum is like running laps and doing drills. Then the team will scrimmage, playing each other on the court while the coach makes comments and yells at them to work harder. Section 1 is the scrimmage, minus the yelling. At the end of the practice, the coach makes the team run wind sprints up and down the gym until they are exhausted while he shouts at them that they're not trying hard enough and they'll never survive the physical demands of a game. Section 2 is like the wind sprints, minus the shouting.

The Big Five Problem Solving Techniques

In 1945 George Poyla wrote a book called "How To Solve It" in which he synthesized thousands of years of research on how mathematicians solve math problems, and which, unfortunately, I didn't discover until 10 years after graduate school. I used the material in How To Solve It to teach engineers how to solve technical problems. One day I simplified the skillset and experimented with kids. After spectacular results, I start math coaching sessions with this skill set for all ages.

Jo Boaler from Stanford takes a similar approach, incorporates soft skills, and does it in a way that is readily accessible to parents. Jo is leading the revolution in math curriculum with a focus (as far as I can tell) on middle school and high school math. I consider the term "Best Practices" in math education synonymous with Boaler's book "Mathematical Mindsets" published in November of 2015. Boaler presents problems, solution techniques, and approaches to teaching math at the middle school level. She has had phenomenal success with inner city kids who are failing in math. If you want to do further research on approaches to problem solving, I recommend starting with Boaler's book.

While this workbook is motivated by recent research in math education, I break from best practices for two important reasons. First, the best practices in math are optimal in a classroom situation with children of mixed abilities, and this workbook is more suitable for an above average child working with a parent for a 3 to 6 month period. Secondly, the purpose of this book is to teach critical thinking skills and problem solving skills at a level that would give your child a substantial advantage in school and on a cognitive skills test under the premise that if your child thinks at a high level, she can teach herself math or any other subject. In short, this workbook is not teaching math, but thinking skills under the premise that the child who masters these skills can teach herself math.

My 1st through 4th grade version of Problem Solving Techniques is a subset of Poyla's full list and includes two of Boaler's recommendations that are directly applicable to children:

1. Be baffled by the problem.

2. Read and understand the problem and use all of the elements of the question.

3. Draw a picture.

4. Decompose the big complicate problem into smaller problems that are easy to solve.

5. Check your work and try again

For middle school students, this list would change. For example, I would add "Translate the hard problem into a much easier one, solve it, gain an understanding, and then try the hard problem". I recommend this technique for a few problems in this workbook, as noted in the solutions. We use this technique any time the child sees really difficult material for the first time, like 92 x 57, or polynomials. It's a powerful way to deeply understand new math at any age. Similarly, techniques for solving advanced math problems would including building on a previously solved problem. In this workbook, I include a bit of repetition and problems that refer to prior problems, but almost all of the problems stand on their own.

With the Big Five in mind, here's how a child goes from slightly above average or worse to the 99th percentile.

1. Two children see the same problem and they are both baffled. One child is "stuck" and gives up. One child either assumes everyone else is baffled or is comfortable with baffled and just plods on. Comfortable with baffled is the starting point for achievement in math and other subjects.

2. School teaches and enforces speed and memorization. Kids skip through

problems quickly. The result is 1 minute reading a problem and 20 minutes getting it wrong. We're going to change this to 15 minutes reading a problem and 1 minute getting wrong anyway and then doing the problem over.

3. A big problem at all ages is missing a key element of a problem, like ignoring new vocabulary word or an implied relationship in the question. The best way to enforce this skill, in my opinion, is to give your child a whole workbook of tricky problems and concentrate on rereading the question.

4. Almost every problem in this book requires problem decomposition, because most problems require solving 2 or 3 equations. A question requiring problem decomposition is a derivative of a question designed to build working memory. Working memory is critical to success in academics and is a consistent theme in this workbook.

5. The difference between a kid in the 85th percentile and the kid in the 99th percentile is that the smarter kid, while no better in math or anything else, simply bothers to check his answers and fix the mistakes. I intentionally designed each problem with simple arithmetic, but it will likely require multiple attempts to get a correct answer. The "redo" is a normal part of this workbook.

This workbook is going to hammer away at these themes on every question.

For some children and parents, the habit of getting a problem incorrect provides benefits way beyond learning to check the work. When your child is comfortable with mistakes, in the sense that the world doesn't come crashing down if they miss 2 problems on a math test, then the child is poised to do great things. The expectation of perfect scores and the reward for "correct" answers can result in unnecessary frustration. I have found that ignoring incorrect answers and not keeping score improves grades. Not caring about incorrect answers and simply requesting a redo improves grades even more.

Keep "Draw A Picture" in your back pocket and use it at your discretion. I prefer that my children try to solve most of the problems mentally and resort to drawing a picture either because they are struggling to understand the question or they've already gotten it wrong 3 times and we are running out of time.

The Third Problem Type

Most of these problems contain some elements of a Reading Comprehension question, including an occasional new vocabulary word, a passage that is challenging to navigate, a passage that requires inference, and the need to reread the passage after reading the question, especially on a question that includes a bonus question.

Before I surveyed the test prep literature and really understood that cognitive skills tests were measuring academic skills, I successfully used reading comprehension questions to prepare for the test. I didn't do this intentionally. I didn't know test prep books existed. After designing lots of test prep questions on my own using circles and squares, I realized that these tests didn't really care whether or not your child was an expert at circles and squares, and I went back to reading comprehension questions for test prep, again with success.

Reading comprehension questions exercise a skills set that is compatible with the one outlined above. Unfortunately, reading comprehension workbooks do not build quantitative skills.

Coaching Advice For Parents

The goals for each question in this workbook are for your child to be baffled, spend a lot of time figuring out what the question is asking, solve multiple equations, get the wrong answer, and then reread the question and try again. In order to meet these goals, you may have to coach math in a different way than you normally do.

The primary goal of school math curriculum is for children to understand and be able to apply math concepts. Most parents respond to their children's request for help by helping the child understand the math concepts by explaining the math concepts. This undermines learning. Instead, your response to a question in this workbook should be bafflement. Your child is baffled, you're baffled, the author's children are complaining, and the author is thinking to himself "what was I thinking when I wrote this problem?"

Typically, the next challenge is to get a child to read the question until it is understood. Most children will expect the teacher, coach, or parent to explain a question, because most of the time the child asks for an explanation and gets one.   Stop doing this.

Be prepared to work with a child for 30 minutes on the first few questions while he reads it over and over again, one word at a time, while he figures out what the question is asking and how to solve it. Initially, this may involve a lot of crying.   How dare you expect your poor child to think for themselves? No one has ever demanded such an outrageous proposition.   If this workbook does nothing more than get each parent to stop helping and teach the child to help themselves, then it succeeded.

You may come across a concept like "20 x 30" when your child has never see "2 x 3" before. In this case, you might have to explain mathematical concepts, but don't explain the question. Take a break from the question and explore the math concepts on their own. Feel free at any time to let the child just draw the question and solve it by counting.

Expect multiple attempts to get a correct answer. Many mistakes will result from the nature of these questions, because the problem requires the child to solve 7 + 7 = 14, 3 + 6 = 9, and 14 – 9 = 5. This is the working memory part. These equations are likely buried in a convoluted goofy problem, and your child might be solving 7 + 8 = 15 when 7 + 7 = 14 is required.   When a child has to solve these 3 equations multiple times to overcome arithmetic errors, you are getting math fact practice as a bonus.

For fear that a child is good at arithmetic, and therefore might not learn build the habit of redoing a problem, for a child who somehow gets past my convoluted question and is poised to get the problem correct on the first try, I added questions like this "Oliver wants to give each of his friends a football. There are 6 kids. How many footballs does he need?" The answer would be 5, since Oliver is one of the kids. This technique looks simple now, but not when surreptitiously buried in a more complicated question.

Some of the bonus questions are added to double the math, some just for fun, some to introduce things for the child to think about but not answer, and some are added to stump the child to ensure that the child gets something wrong the first try. Unless the bonus question requires a secondary calculation on par with the average question, we typically don't redo bonus questions but just debate them. Feel free to let your child be correct on the goofier bonus questions if your child disputes the solution.

To summarize my advice: be baffled, don't help, and don't care about incorrect answers. If your child is making zero progress, after your child has read the question multiple times, jump in as the missing team member and help. Expect your effort to diminish over time as your child's skills improve.

The ideal math workbook produces extraordinary results with no involvement or time commitment from the parent. The ideal math workbook hasn't been invented yet. This workbook will take 30 to 45 minutes of parent time per question until your child learns to read question on his own without complaining, and then at least 10 minutes per question after that saying things like "read the question again" and "try again, you missed something".

For more advice, feel free to post questions or complaints to my blog, www.getyourchildintogat.com.

Question 1

Hannah just turned 3. Hannah's mom made a birthday cake for Hannah, and Hannah's older brother Oliver put enough candles on the birthday cake for his age plus 4 extra candles that he found in the box. How many candles did Hannah's mom have to take off of the cake if Oliver is 10 years old?

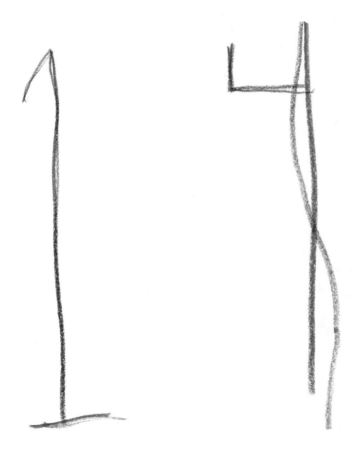

Question 2

Hannah found 9 green hats and 6 pink hats in a box next to the front door. Hannah put 6 hats on her dolls and 8 hats on her stuffed animals. When Oliver went to the hat box to get a hat, what did he find in the hat box?

Question 3

Oliver asked Hannah to put the hats back in the hat box. Her 6 dolls are wearing hats and her 8 stuffed animals are wearing hats. She took hats off of the stuffed animals and put them back into the box. Now only 3 stuffed animals are wearing hats. She took an equal number of hats off of her dolls. Now how many dolls and stuffed animals are wearing hats?

Question 4

Oliver found a sweater for an octopus in his closet. He also found pants for an octopus in the closet.   The sweater and the pants have the same number of arms and legs, because an octopus wears a sweater or pants but not both. If Oliver put on the pants and the sweater, how many sweater arms and pant legs do not have an arm or a leg in them?

Bonus Question: Why does Oliver have a sweater and pants for an octopus in his closet that fit him?

Question 5

Oliver asked his mother for a snack. Oliver's mother cut an apple into 8 slices. Some of the slices had a single seed and the rest of the slices did not have a seed. How many more slices have a seed than don't have a seed?

Question 6

The Supreme Court of the United States has donut day every Tuesday. It is the official responsibility of the Clerk of the Court to bring donuts. The Clerk brought a dozen donuts. 6 of these donuts were not frosted. The justices in the court like frosted donuts and are not happy if they did not get a frosted donut. How many justices at the Supreme Court are not happy on donut day?

Bonus Question: How would your answer change if the Clerk ate 2 of the donuts while driving from the donut shop to the court building?

Super Bonus Question: If the clerk didn't eat any donuts, how can he make the unhappy justices happy again without having to go back to the donut shop?

Question 7

Hannah's neighbor gave Hannah a daisy and six roses. Her neighbor has a big garden. Each rose has 6 petals and there are lots of petals on the daisy. The daisies in this garden have between 21 and 34 petals on each flower. If Hannah ate all of the petals off of one rose, does she have more rose petals than daisy petals?

Bonus Question: Is it OK to eat rose petals?

Super Bonus Question: Does Hannah's neighbor have pickles in her garden?

Question 8

Mallory found instructions to make paper mantes in a book about origami. She wanted to make 200 paper mantes. Lilly and Yani offered to help. Mallory asked Lily to make 100 paper mantes and she asked Yani to make 50 more. How paper mantes will Mallory make?

Bonus Question: If it takes 2 pieces of paper to make a mantis, how many pieces of paper does Mallory need?

Question 9

Mallory has an enormous bag of pom poms. She fills boxes with pom poms and gives the boxes to Yani and Lily. The first box can fit in the second box, and the second box can fit in the third box, and the third box can fit in the fourth box. Which boxes should Mallory give to Lily and Yani so that each person has about the same number of pom poms?

Bonus Question: If the first 3 boxes can fit in the fourth box with their lids on, how does this change your answer?

Super Bonus Question: Why is Mallory giving Yani and Lily pom poms?

Question 10

Yani and Mallory went skating. Their 3 friends, Lily, Soren, and Bowen sat in the stands and rated the performances. Yani received a 5 from Lily, a 6 from Soren, and a 9 from Bowen.   Mallory received an 8 from Lily, a 4 from Soren, and her total score was higher than Yani's score. What score did Bowen give Mallory?

Question 11

Oliver and Kai are playing frisbee golf. Oliver threw the frisbee 9 yards on his first try and 6 yards on his second try.   Kai threw the frisbee 7 yards on his first try and 12 yards on his second try. If the frisbee net is 30 yards from where they started, who is closer?

Bonus question: How much closer?

Question 12

The red lipped batfish collects lipstick that people accidentally drop in the ocean. The red lipped batfish puts each lipstick in a shell. One red lipped batfish has 5 shells and 3 lipsticks. She swam around and found 4 more lipsticks. How many more shells does she need for the lipsticks?

Question 13

Kai and his sister Hannah groomed their cats. It takes 7 minutes to comb the hair of the first cat. The second cat is twice as big. How long will it take to comb the hair of both cats?

Question 14

Hannah and Kai have a stack of pennies and pieces of cardboard. Hannah's piece of cardboard is a circle and Kai's piece of cardboard is a square. The pieces of cardboard are the same size. Hannah said "Since my piece is a circle, I can fit more pennies on it that your piece." The children cover the cardboard with one layer of pennies. The pennies are not stacked on top of each other. The pieces of cardboard are about 7 inches wide.

Explain why Hannah is not correct.

Question 15

Hanna collected all of the pennies from the previous problem and counted them. Hannah had 8 pennies and Kai had 13 pennies. Oliver reached into his pocket and found four coins. Oliver counted his coins and found out that he had as much money as Hanna. What were the coins in Oliver's pocket? Draw them.

Question 16

Hannah has a cat named "Fur Blob" who is really lazy. Fur Blob didn't move for 5 days. Every day, a mouse brought Fur Blob 2 pieces of cheese. If the mouse started with 20 pieces of cheese, and the mouse ate 1 piece of cheese each day, how many pieces of cheese does the mouse have left after the five days?

Bonus Question: What is the problem with a cat who doesn't move for five days?

Question 17

Fur Blob appreciated the cheese that the mouse brought him. To show his gratitude, the cat decided to make a bed for the mouse out of matchboxes. There were 32 matches in the match box. The cat had to wait until the match box was empty. Oliver's family lights a fire with the matches every other night. Half the time, it takes 2 matches to light the fire, and half the time it takes 1 match to light the fire. If 2 matches were used to light a fire tonight, how many days must the mouse wait until she can sleep on a bed?

Bonus Question: If Oliver's family lights the fire with 1 match tonight, how much longer must the mouse wait for a bed?

Super Bonus Question: How many matches does the family use each day?

Question 18

Kai had a dream that he was stranded on a desert island for all of January. On the desert island, he found a microwave and 80 microwave burritos. If he ate a burrito for breakfast, lunch and dinner, how many meals did he have to eat coconuts instead?

Bonus Question: On how many days did Kai eat coconuts in this dream?

Question 19

The Giant Gippsland earthworm can grow up to 10 feet in length. If this earthworm is cut in half, each half will grow into a full sized worm. If you take a Giant Gippsland earthworm and cut it in half, and then cut each piece in half again, and they all grow up, how many feet of earthworms will there be altogether?

Bonus Question: What happens if you cut a Giant Gippsland earthworm in half?

Question 20

Oliver made 4 cheese and cracker kabobs. He cut 18 pieces of cheese and had 19 crackers. If he makes each kabob as equal as possible, how much more cheese and crackers does the kabob with the most have than the kabob with the least?

Bonus Question: If Oliver has 7 oranges and 14 cans of soda, how many wheels does he have on his skateboard?

Question 21

Oliver decided to make Cheese and Cracker Kabobs to sell. He bought 8 boxes and wrote "Oliver's Cheese and Cracker Kabobs" on each box. Then he drew a UPC symbol on the back. He had enough cheese slices to put 4 slices of cheese in each box. He has 44 crackers, and puts as many crackers in each box as he can, and each box has the same number of crackers. How many more crackers does he have in all of his boxes than pieces of cheese?

Bonus Question: Oliver took his 8 boxes of Cheese and Cracker Kabobs to the grocery store and asked the manager if the store would put the boxes on a shelf and sell them. What did the store manager ask Oliver?

Question 22

Oliver lives down the street from a fire station. The fire station has 3 trucks, and the siren on each truck makes a different sound.

On one busy day, Oliver heard the fire chief's car go out on 8 calls. The small fire truck followed the fire chief six times, and the truck with the big ladder followed the fire chief 3 times. The small truck went out on 7 more calls without the fire chief. The big truck with the ladder never goes out unless it follows the fire chief's car. On this day, how many more times did the small truck go out on a call than the big truck with the ladder?

Bonus Question: If Oliver can't see the trucks from his house, how does he know which truck is going out on a call?

Question 23

Hannah built a fort out of couch cushions. The couch has 8 big cushions and 7 small cushions. If she uses big cushions for 3 walls and the roof, and 4 of the small cushions for the front wall of her fort, how many more big cushions than small cushions are left on the couch?

Bonus Question: If Oliver jumps on the cushion fort, what is Hannah left with?

Question 24

Mallory watched her siblings play in a coach pitch little league game. It was a two inning game. In the first inning, Mallory's sister Sophie hit a home run and her team scored 4 other runs. In the second inning, Sophie's brother scored twice and 6 other kids on the team scored once. The other team scored 7 times in the first inning and 6 times in the second inning. A mom asked Mallory who won the game. What was Mallory's answer?

Question 25

Oliver visited a farm. At the farm, he saw a drift numbering 20 in a pen. He came back an hour later, and the drift was only 3.   He saw 8 of the baby pigs in a barn.   How many of the drift is still missing?

Question 26

Lilly has a neighbor named Sumi Von Gusa. One day, she saw Sumi Von Gusa sitting in front of his house with a circus clown next to a bag of magic peanuts. "What are you doing?" she asked. Sumi Von Gusa replied, "This clown lost an elephant and a monkey. I made a batch of magic peanuts and magic bananas which will bring all the monkeys and elephants in town here." 5 zoo elephants and 7 circus elephants stopped by, and 9 zoo monkeys and 5 circus monkeys stopped by. They fed each animal a peanut or a banana, how many more bananas were eaten than peanuts?

Bonus question: How many fewer magic bananas does Sumi Von Gusa have than magic peanuts?

Question 27

Yani lives in a family with 13 kids and 2 parents. They sit at a round table. The parents sit next to each other. Every night, each parent brings a pot of peas to the table. Each pot has 7 servings of peas and a big spoon in it. The parent serves themselves, and then pass the pot to the nearest kid. By the time the pots reach Yani, they are both empty.   Where does Yani sit? Draw a picture.

Bonus Question: Does Yani like peas?

Question 28

Yani, Oliver, Lily and Mallory are played a game of popcorn dash. Yani threw 11 buckets of popcorn to Mallory, but she spilled 8 of the buckets. Lily threw 18 buckets of popcorn to Oliver but he spilled 13 of them. Birds ate one of the buckets of popcorn that Oliver didn't spill. The team with the most buckets of popcorn won. Who won?

Bonus Question: Where do you think they are playing this game? Make a list of possible places.

Question 29

In the back of Yani's house is a big garden where his mom plants corn. Yani decided that he wants to plant peas so that he can find out what peas taste like. The garden has room for 30 corn stalks, but Yani's mom only has 24 corn seeds. Yani has a bag of 12 pea seeds and he plans to plant a pea seed in each spot where his mom does not plant a corn seed. How many pea seeds will Yani have left after both Yani and his mom are finished planting?

Question 30

Hannah's cat has 9 little stuffed mouse toys. Hannah decides to make felt eyebrows for the mouse toys and glue them on. She can cut 3 eyebrows out of a piece of gray felt, and she has 5 pieces of gray felt. How many stuffed mouse toys are not going to get eyebrows?

Question 31

Oliver's Cheese and Cracker Kabob idea was a big hit. The grocery store manager from Question #21 agreed to sell the 8 boxes and the boxes sold on the first day.   All grocery stores in the nation wanted to sell them, so Oliver rented a warehouse, hired 100 workers, and sold Cheese and Cracker Kabobs to grocery stores for $2.00 each.   In the first year, Oliver made $3,000,000. His parents told him that he can only keep enough money to buy a PS4 for $400, and he has to divide the rest of the money equally among his workers. One of his workers is Hannah, and she made a total of 17 Cheese and Cracker Kabob boxes in her bedroom. How much money did Hannah get?

Bonus Question: Guess how many PS4's Hannah can buy with her money and then check with a calculator.

Super Bonus Question: Is this fair?

Question 32

Oliver's neighbor Yani was impressed with Oliver's success, so Yani decided to start a candy company. His product was called British Salmon Candy, which is just Swedish fish in a new package. He bought 100 bags of Swedish fish for $2.00 each. A packaging company sold him 200 empty packaging bags printed with "British Salmon Candy by Yani" on the front with a British flag and a professional looking UPC code in the bottom right for 25 cents each. Yani bought a $30 machine to seal each bag. He put half a bag of Swedish fish in each of his British Salmon bags. Will Yani make any money on this product? He will sell each package for $3.00.

Bonus Question: Draw a package of British Salmon Candy.

Super Bonus Question: Would you buy a bag of British Salmon Candy from Yani?

Question 33

Yani, Oliver, Lily and Mallory go to a movie theater. Yani and Oliver want to see the movie Return of the Zoomies, but Lily and Mallory want to see Space Flight 3000.   At the theater showing Return of the Zoomies, the tickets cost $3 and each box of candy cost $2.50. At the theater showing Space Flight 3000, the tickets cost $4 and each box of candy cost $1.50. If each child wants a box of candy, and Mallory's mom gives the children $21, what should they do?   None of the children has any other money than the money that Mallory's mom gave them.

Bonus Question: Suppose Yani wants to see the movie Return of the Zoomies more than anything.   What can he do to convince Mallory and Lily to see this movie?

Question 34

Oliver licked a big lollipop. He will need to lick the lollipop 5,193,879 times before it is all gone. So far, he licked it 4 times. How many more times will he need to lick it?

Bonus Question: Can you calculate how many more licks Oliver has left if he licked the lollipop 950 times?

Question 35

Yani's grandmother came to visit from Romania for 3 weeks. When she visits, she sleeps in his bedroom and he sleeps under the dining room table. Yani counts the days until he gets to sleep in his bed. 5 days after his grandmother arrived, how many more days does he have to sleep under the dining room table?

Bonus Question: What is Yani sleeping on?

Question 36

Yani's grandmother wakes up every morning at 4 am to make chimney cakes. Her chimney cakes each have 6 layers. If she made 4 chimney cakes on Monday and 3 chimney cakes on Tuesday, and Yani's family ate 5 chimney cakes on Tuesday night, how many chimney cakes will she have to make on Wednesday so that there are 24 layers when Yani wakes up on Wednesday morning?

Question 37

Oliver and Hannah visited the Statue of Liberty in New York City. There were 2 lines going into the statue. They wanted to choose the shortest line. The first line had 19 people, and then 9 went inside. The second line had only 6 people, but 5 more people got in that line. Which line should they choose?

Bonus Question: Draw one version of this problem with the Statue of Liberty, the building it sits on, and stick figures going to the statue. Draw another version of this problem just using circles. You can cross out the circles that went inside.

Question 38

Kai and Hannah are standing in line at the Metropolitan Museum of Art. They feel like they've spent their whole trip to New York standing in line. There are 12 people standing in front of them and 8 people standing behind them. 3 people go in and 8 more join the end of the line. How many more people are behind them in line than in front of them?

Bonus Question: If Kai and Hannah have to go to the bathroom, and lose their place in line, how does this change your answer?

Question 39

Eleanor Sincomhoff works at a company that makes microwave ovens. To test each microwave oven, she makes a package of microwave popcorn and a cup of tea in each oven. One day, she made 15 bags of popcorn in big microwaves and 18 bags in small microwaves. Three of the microwaves didn't work at all when popping popcorn. Eleanor dumped each bag into a bucket and stacked each bucket out back next to the dumpster. The other workers stopped by to chat with Eleanor and have a cup of hot tea. There were 9 cups of tea that nobody drank. How many workers are there at this company?

Bonus Question: Did you guess where Yani, Oliver, Lily and Mallory were playing their game in Question #28?

Super Bonus Question: After the game of popcorn dash, how many buckets of popcorn are left next to the dumpster?

Question 40

Oliver was sick on Tuesday and missed a math test. When he went to school on Wednesday, his teacher Mr. Bill Nilson gave him a make-up test during recess. Oliver noticed that Bill watches him write his answers. When Oliver gets the wrong answer, Bill stares with "Big Eyebrows".

Bill gives super hard tests. Any kid who gets more than half correct gets an A. There are 100 questions on the test. On 35 questions, Bill looked with "furrowed" eyebrows, and on 10 questions, Bill looked at Oliver with one big Eyebrow and the other one furrowed. The rest of the time Oliver got big eyebrows from Bill on each question. Did Oliver miss more than half of the questions?

Bonus Question: Practice staring at a mirror with "big eye brows". First, make a grumpy face. Then, while grumpy looking, raise your eyebrows as high as they will go. Try furrowing your brow, otherwise known as "low brows". Try raising a single eye brow and lowering the other one. Next, have an argument with one of your family members where you don't speak but just use different "eyebrow superpowers". Did you win the argument?

Question 41

Lily and her brother Ivan stood with their baseball team waiting for rides. Parents with SUVs are going to pick them up to take them to the championship game. There are 12 other kids on the team. If Lily's older sister Mallory is coming, and each SUV seats 5 people (with gear in the back), what is the fewest number of people who are going to this game and how many SUVs are needed?

Yani watched a video about a cup stacking competition. In the video, the 10 year old world champion cup stacker made 2 pyramids of 3 cups each, and a pyramid of 6 cups, all at the same time. Yani found 8 blue cups in the cupboard and 3 red cups in the bathroom. Does he have enough cups so that each pyramid would only have one color of cup?

Question 43

Mallory and Yani are in the Recycle Club at school. They are collecting plastic shopping bags. If a Recycle Club member brings in 50 plastic shopping bags, the member will earn the Super Recycler badge.   Yani found 20 bags in the woods and 25 bags at the park. Mallory found 20 bags on her street and 50 bags at the grocery store. Did the kids earn the Super Recycler badge?

Bonus Question: The children walk to the club meeting together. When they get there, they both earn the badge. What happened?

Question 44

Yani and Mallory each earned a bag of candy from the Recycling Club for collecting plastic bags. Yani has a bag of licorice with 30 pieces. Mallory has a bag of chocolate with 25 bars. If Yani traded 15 licorice pieces for 12 chocolate bars, how many more licorice pieces does Yani have than Mallory has chocolate bars?

Bonus Question: After the other kids saw that the Recycling Club is giving away badges for collecting bags, 534 children signed up for the Recycling Club and started collecting bags. There were no more discarded plastic bags anywhere in the town. Oliver wants to collect bags to earn his Recycling Club badge. What is he going to do?

Super Bonus Question: The bonus question said that children want to join the Recycling Club to earn a badge. What is the real reason children want to join the Recycling Club?

Question 45

One night in November, Oliver's parents didn't have time to cook. Oliver, Kai, and Hannah decided to order a pizza with olives. The pizza cost 13 dollars plus 3 dollars extra for the olives. Oliver and Kai had 7 dollars each that they can use to purchase the pizza. How much money do they need from Hannah to order the pizza?

Bonus Question: If Hannah only has 3 Canadian dollars and 1 US dollar, can they still get the pizza?

Question 46

Yani's family has a chicken coop in the back yard. There are 9 white chickens that laid 2 eggs each.   The brown chickens laid 1/3 the eggs that the white chickens laid and the yellow chickens laid 5 eggs. Are there enough eggs so that each person in Yani's family can have 2?

Question 47

Yani went back to his chicken coop to visit his favorite chicken, a yellow chicken named Butterscotch. This chicken is Yani's favorite because it is the only yellow chicken. The others are either brown or white. The chickens all left the coop and were wandering around the garden. Yani brought back all 9 white chickens but only 7 of the brown chickens. If 3 of the white chickens ran back into the garden, and there are 14 chickens in the chicken coop, is Butterscotch in the coop?

Bonus Question: If Yani has 10 brown chickens, how many more chickens are in the coop than in the garden?

Super Bonus Question: Yani decided to rename his yellow chicken. What is another good name for a yellow chicken?

Question 48

Jeffrey Sincomhoff delivers pizza. One night, he had to deliver a pizza, but he forgot which house on the street ordered the pizza. He knew that the house that was exactly in the middle of the block. On one side of the street, there were 8 white houses and 4 yellow houses.   On the other side of the street, there were 6 brick houses, 7 wooden houses, and 2 houses made out of loaves of whole wheat bread.   All of the houses and the yards were exactly the same size. How did he know which house ordered the pizza?

Bonus Question: Was it possible that the house is made out of whole wheat bread?

Question 49

Yani wants to collect all of the Zoomie action figures from season 1 and season 2 of the show "Zoomies". There are 10 different Zoomie action figures from season one and 12 different Zoomie action figures from season two. Yani has 6 Zoomie action figures from season one and 9 action figures from season two. For his 10th birthday, he got a package of 6 Zoomie action figures. He already had 3 of the action figures in this package. How many more Zoomie action figures does he need to complete his collection?

Bonus Question: Draw a Zoomie.

Question 50

Sumi Von Gusa had to go on a trip, so he asked Oliver and Hannah to watch his 12 Penguins. Oliver's dad put a big freezer in the basement and left the door open so it would be cold. Hannah got all of the hats from question #2. If there are 7 girl penguins, and Hannah puts a hat on each one, and she puts a hat on 2 of the boy penguins, how many green hats are not on a penguin's head?

Bonus Question: It is possible that Hanna did not put all 6 pink hats on the girl penguins. What are the other possibilities for green hats not worn?

Question 51

Yani pulled weeds in his garden on a Saturday morning. Under a very big weed, he found a map to the temple of Zoomirantuk. The map is a picture of his garden with little circles and a big "X" in the middle. The writing on the map said "Follow the path with the fewest stones and there you will find the temple." He pulled some more weeds and found a path of square stones. There were 10 square blue stones and 7 square red stones. About 10 feet away he saw a path of round stones. This path had 8 round yellow stones and 8 round green stones.

Draw the map. Which path should he take to find the temple of Zoomirantuk?

Question 52

Kai went to camp to learn archery. He was not good at archery. The first time he tried it, he shot 20 arrows and only hit the target 3 times. Jeffrey Sincomhoff is a camper who is good at archery. Jeffrey shot 18 arrows and hit the target 14 times. How many more times did Kai miss than Jeffrey?

Question 53

Oliver thinks that there are monsters in his bedroom closet, so he goes to the library to learn everything he can about monsters. He checked out 17 DVDs about monsters, but only watched 9 of them, and checked out 18 books about monsters but only read 5 of them. How many more DVDs did he watch than books that he read?

Bonus Questions: Of all of the monsters there are, which ones like to live in Oliver's stinky boring closet?

Question 54

Yani is practicing stacking cups.   In order to qualify for competition, he has to be able to stack 3 pyramids of cups in 5 seconds or less. On Monday, his worst time was 15 seconds when the cat jumped on the table, and his best time was 8 seconds. On Tuesday, his worst time was 12 seconds and his best time was 7 seconds. Between Monday and Tuesday, how much did the difference between his best and worst times change?

Bonus Question: Get 12 cups and see how quickly you can stack and unstack them into the 3 pyramids used by the 3-6-3 cup stacking competition.

Question 55

Hannah plays with an old piano. It is smaller than a regular piano and only has room for 61 keys. 7 of the white keys are missing. If this piano has 25 black keys, how many more white keys does it have than black keys?

Bonus Question: Draw the keyboard. If you play the piano, do not look at your piano and draw the keyboard anyway. If you don't play the piano, consider playing the Clarinet when you are in the fourth grade.

Question 56

Hannah decided to fix her piano from the last question. Each white key is 5 inches long and 1 inch wide. Her dad offers to go to the hardware store to buy a saw and the wood she will need to make the keys. He asks Hannah how much wood he should buy. The hardware store sells strips of wood 1 inch wide and the perfect depth for piano keys. What does Hannah say?

Bonus Question: Hannah takes apart her piano and finds out that each key is 15 inches long. The part of the key that shows is 5 inches, and the rest is hidden in the piano. How much more wood should he buy than Hannah's original request?

Super Bonus Question: When Hannah cut the 1 wide inch board down the long end to make 7 boards that are 15 inches long, the last key was ½ an inch short. What happened? Hint: You may need to look at a saw to figure this out.

Question 57

Hannah's piano is finally fixed and she decides to start practicing regularly. In the first half of the month, she practiced 12 days. In the second half of the month, she practiced 9 days. If this month is June, how many more days off did she take in the second half of the month than the first?

Bonus Question: Is Hannah practicing regularly?

Question 58

Kai is determined to become an expert archer. At 4:00 pm on a Monday, Kai found a stack of 16 cups in the back yard of Yani's house. Kai lined up the cups on a table, took out 16 arrows, and started shooting arrows at the cups. The first time he tried it, he missed 11 of the cups. Seven hours later, on the 119th time he tried it, he only missed 4 of the cups. How many more cups did he hit on the 119th time than the first time?

Bonus Question: Kai is happy with his hard work and improvement. Who is not happy?

Question 59

Yani and Mallory made origami figures in art class. Yani made an origami pig and an origami chicken and showed them to Mallory. Mallory ripped the origami pig into 11 pieces and the origami chicken into 13 pieces, and then threw the pieces out the window. Yani went outside and found most of the pieces, and then he glued them together. The pig is missing 3 pieces and the chicken is missing 5 pieces. How many pieces did Yani find?

Question 60

Yani practiced for the cup stacking competition. On Monday, he practiced for 35 minutes, but he spent 23 of those minutes complaining about how hard it is. On Tuesday, he practiced for 29 minutes, but he spent 15 minutes complaining that his arms were tired. How much more time did he practice on Tuesday than Monday?

Bonus Question: What can Yani do better when he is practicing?

Question 61

Mallory is learning how to build robots. Her first robot was a robot copy of Lily.   Mallory didn't tighten all of the bolts enough. When Lily Robot walked down the street, her pieces fell apart. Each piece requires 3 bolts. Mallory found the arms, legs, hands, and feet, plus two hip parts and the torso. The only piece she didn't find was the head. Mallory found 7 bolts and the real Lily found 3 bolts. How many bolts are missing?

Bonus Question: Find a nut and a matching bolt. Create a math question based on the nut and the bolt. The math question has to be a real one and can't be a goofy made up question like the ones in this book.

Question 62

Oliver and his brother and sister went to see a jazz big band perform. The band had 19 members. 13 of these members played brass instruments. There were only 13 people in the audience. Six audience members liked brass. How many people are at this jazz concert who either play an instrument that is not brass or don't like brass instruments?

Question 63

The Recycling Club had a fund raiser. The children sold reusable paper cups for 25 cents each and special commemorative cups for a dollar each. Yani sold 20 paper cups and 7 commemorative cups. Mallory sold 8 paper cups and twice as many commemorative cups as Yani. How many more commemorative cups does Yani have to sell so that he earns more than Mallory? First, figure out how many reusable paper cups must be sold to equal a commemorative cup.

Bonus Question: Did Yani sell more commemorative cups than Mallory?

Question 64

Yani accidentally recycled all of the clubs registration forms. There are 13 girls and 9 boys in the club. If 3 girls didn't turn in their registration forms, and Mallory found 8 registration forms in the recycling bin, what is the largest possible number of registration forms for the boys that are still missing?

Bonus question: If 4 of the registration forms that Mallory found are for boys, how many more girls are missing registration forms than boys?

Question 65

Hannah played a video game called Tap the Banana. When a banana appeared on the screen, Hannah tapped it, and got a gold coin. Gold coins can be used to buy bananas. Bananas never disappear unless tapped. While Hannah played, 14 bananas appeared. She tapped 9 of these and bought 5 bananas with the gold coins. 6 more bananas appeared and she tapped 3 of these. How many bananas are on the screen?

Bonus Question: How many fewer gold coins does Hannah have than bananas?

Super Bonus Question: Hannah's older brother Oliver walked by and Hannah asked him what he thought of the game. What did Oliver reply?

Question 66

Yani's big family is very loud but Yani is very quiet. The parents created "Dojo points" to reward being quiet. Each kid gets Dojo points for being quiet, and at the end of the month, any kid with 100 or more Dojo points gets a slurpee. In the first few weeks of February, Yani's parents gave out 120 Dojo points, but Yani got 70 of these. In the last 2 weeks of February, Yani got 60 Dojo points and the rest of his brothers and sisters got 80 Dojo points all together. How many more dojo points did Yani get in February than the rest of his family?

Bonus Question: How many slurpees did his parents buy for their children at the end of February?

Super Bonus Question: If Yani's parents bought 2 slurpees in February, what is the biggest possible number of Dojo points earned by children who didn't get a Slurpee?

Question 67

Lily went to the doctor. She had to wait an hour for the doctor. Lily hates to wait because it is boring. Lily's Dad suggested that Lily make a list of things to do while she waits. Lilly decided that she can spend 12 minutes doodling on a pieces of paper, 12 minutes making up a song about apricots, and 20 minutes thinking about the boring boringness of boredom. If the doctor was 7 minutes early, how much more time does Lily need on her list of things to do so that she is busy the whole time she is waiting?

Question 68

NASA had a competition to choose the first child to ride on the space shuttle. The rules of the competition were a) to be 10 years old and b) write a winning essay on "How you faced a challenge and things turned out good anyway." Yani entered the competition with an essay.

This is what Yani wrote: "I am 10 years old. My challenge is that a girl named Mallory beats me at everything. Last month, she beat me at 7 games of kick ball on the playground and 4 games of dodge ball in gym. She beat me at 6 games of Monopoly at home and 9 games of baseball in the park next to our house. If I win this competition by having the worst challenge, then it will turn out good."

How many fewer times did Mallory beat him last month at school than other places?

Bonus Question: Did Yani win the competition?

Question 69

Oliver wanted to get each of the children in his class a stuffed Zoomie elk ornament. He found 22 stuffed Zoomie elks at the first store, but 8 of these didn't light up. There were 11 stuffed Zoomie elks at another store. If there are 28 kids in Oliver's class, does he have enough?

Bonus Question: If Oliver was willing to buy Zoomie elk ornaments that don't light up, how many did he give that didn't light up?

Question 70

Yani lives on the same block as Sumi Von Gusa. Sumi Von Gusa has a collection of gold coins.   Sumi has 20 gold coins now. When he has a total of 25 gold coins, he will sell his collection.   One morning, Sumi checks his collection and finds that 9 of the gold coins have disappeared. He counted again, and this time 4 of the missing gold coins reappeared and then 3 disappeared again. How many more gold coins does he need to get now so that he can sell his collection?

Bonus Question: Why do Sumi Von Gusa's gold coins keep disappearing and reappearing?

Super Bonus Question: Read question about the Tap the Banana game that Hannah is playing from a previous question, compare it to this question, and then answer the Bonus Question.

Question 71

Mallory made a new Lily Robot that is much better than the first Lily Robot. Lily Robot went to school with Mallory and Lily. In their class, there are 28 kids. 18 of them are girls. Their teacher counted the kids and noticed that there were 29 and not 28. The teacher said "I want half of the boys to stand on the north wall and half of the boys to stand on the south wall. Then I want half of the girls to stand on the east wall and half of the girls to stand on the west wall. Anyone else can stand in a corner." The Lily Robot stood in the corner with girls on the right and boys on the left. How many more girls are standing on the wall next to Lily Robot than boys standing on the other wall next to Lily Robot?

Bonus Question: Without rereading the question, close your book and answer this question: How many more kids are standing on the walls next to Lily Robot than the walls across from Lily Robot?

Question 72

Kai asked Hannah if he could have a turn playing her video game box. He finds a game called "Tap the Seed". In this game, the player taps the seed and it turns into a fruit. If the player taps the fruit, it turns into a vegetable. Next door, Yani's mom is in the garden. She watches as 8 carrots disappear and then 12 heads of lettuce disappear. Then 5 of the carrots come back and 7 of the heads of lettuce come back. How many vegetables appear on Kai's screen?

Super Bonus Question: Kai hears a knock on the door. Yani's mom and Sumi Von Gusa are standing at the door. They don't look happy. Kai's mother answers the door. Yani's mom and Sumi Von Gusa talk quietly with Kai's mom. Then Kai's mom does something. What does Kai's mom do next?

Question 73

Before Sumi Von Gusa left, he saw Yani staring at his unusual pants. "These are my corn peel pants," said Sumi Von Gusa. "Every time I shuck an ear of corn, I save 4 ear leaves and sew them together. I used leaves from 7 ears of corn on my left pant leg, and leaves from 4 ears of corn on my right leg." His pants were tucked into his socks. How many more ear leaves are on his left pant leg than his right pant leg?

Bonus Question: What is different between Sumi Von Gusa's left sock and the right sock?

Question 74

Yani won the space competition. One of the astronauts who is going on this flight is sick and can't go on the trip, so NASA awarded a trip to the second place winner of the space competition. The second place winner was a girl named Mallory who wrote an essay titled "The Challenge of Having a Friend Who Always Loses at Everything". Both Mallory and Yani went to space.

When they were floating around in space, Yani opened a box of food. The box contained tubes of meat and tubes of peas, and these tubes started floating around the space shuttle. Yani grabbed 4 tubes of meat and 9 tubes of peas. Mallory grabbed 8 tubes of peas, 2 tubes of meat, and 4 tubes of oatmeal. All of the tubes were back in the box. How many tubes were there?

Bonus Question: Who grabbed more tubes of food?

Question 75

Yani is really excited about cup stacking. In his bedroom, he has 17 pictures of people taped to his wall, and 9 of these are cup stacking champions. He has 23 other pictures on his wall, and 11 of these are pictures of cups. How many pictures on his wall have nothing to do with cup stacking?

Bonus Question: 3 of other pictures that are not people are pictures of tables. How does this change your answer?

Question 76

Lily is reading a book series called Super Cool Animals. The first book in the series shows pictures of 6 birds and 7 furry cows. The second book in the series shows pictures of 7 monkeys, 5 horses, and 3 birds.   In these pictures, how many fewer eyes are in the first book than the second book?

Bonus Question: Which book has more ears in the pictures?

Question 77

Sumi Von Gusa is a wizard and inventor. He is also Oliver's uncle. Sumi Von Gusa was the one who created the video games that make things disappear. He is slightly crazy and his inventions don't always work. For Hannah's birthday, he gave her a tea set that he called "self-refilling". When a cup of water is poured from the tea pot into a cup, 2 more cups of water magically appear in the pot to take its place. At Hannah's birthday party, she set the table with 6 cups for herself and her friends. She filled the pot to the top with 8 cups of water, and then filled each of the cups. How much water is either in a cup or on the table?

Bonus Question: How much more water is in a cup or on the table than is in the pot?

Super Bonus Question: What is the most water Hannah could put in the pot before she starts filling cups so that none spills on the table?

Question 78

Yani entered the cup stacking competition. He received 15 tickets for his parents, brothers, and sisters for the event. If only 8 of his brothers and sisters can go to the competition, does he have enough tickets to invite his 3 neighbors (Kai, Hannah, and Oliver) and 3 of his friends?

Bonus Question: Does Yani have enough extra tickets to also invite his 2 cats?

Question 79

One day, Hannah's class flew kites.   The girls flew 6 red kites and 9 yellow kites.   3 of the yellow kites got tangled in tree branches.   The boys flew 12 blue kites and 8 of the blue kites did not get tangled up in a tree. How many more blue kites are flying than yellow kites?

Bonus Question: Why is this question silly?

Question 80

To help Oliver practice spelling, Sumi Von Gusa gave him a watch that beeps every time someone misspells a word. It only beeps 15 times a day and then it stops beeping the rest of the day. Oliver took his watch to the spelling bee. The watch had not beeped that day until the spelling bee. Before Oliver's turn, the watch beeped 8 times when 8 kids misspelled words. After his turn, the watch beeped 6 times. Finally, the judge was angry. He said, "If I hear that watch beep again, the owner of the watch has to leave." That would be very embarrassing. There is no off button on the watch. Should Oliver be worried?

Question 81

Lily is going to the store to buy Dinking Binky Trolls. She has 14 quarters and 4 dollars. Each Dinking Binky Troll cost 50 cents. How many Dinky Binky Trolls can she buy if she first stops at a vending machine and buys an Orange Soda for $1.25? Find a clever way to solve this problem so that you don't have to do a lot of calculating.

Bonus Question: Guess what the bonus question is and solve it.

Question 82

Behind Yani's neighborhood is a dark forest. One day, Yani was walking in the forest collecting berries. He had 5 cowberries and 9 strawberries. He was approached by a hooded wizard with the complete set of Zoomie action figures. The hooded wizard told Yani that he would give him the Zoomie action figures if Yani could give him 25 berries. Yani saw a Bilberry bush with 14 Bilberries on it. If he picks the bilberries, how many more berries will Yani need?

Bonus Question: Where is this forest?

Super Bonus Question: Why is there a hooded figure in this forest who is carrying a complete set of Zoomie action figures?

Question 83

Oliver went Trick-Or-Treating on his block. He dressed as an octopus. There are 19 houses on his block. At the first 9 houses, he got 4 Honey Bites and at the other houses, he got 3 Honey Bites. If half of all houses in the rest his neighborhood are giving out Honey Bites, how many more houses does Oliver have to go to so that he gets 25 candies that aren't Honey Bites?

Bonus Question: What are Honey Bites?

Question 84

Yani went Trick-Or-Treating on Oliver's block. He received 8 Polish Lobster Candies. He received 11 Polish Lobster Candies on other blocks in the neighborhood.   If Oliver only got Honey Bites and Polish Lobster Candy while Trick-Or-Treating, how many fewer Polish Lobster Candies did Yani get than Oliver?

Question 85

Kai and Hannah made sandwiches for lunch. They had 18 slices of turkey and 17 slices of roast beef. Kai put 11 slices of turkey on his sandwich. Hannah put 10 slices of roast beef on her sandwich. If they used all of the slices of both types of meat, how many more slices did Kai put on his sandwich than Hannah?

Question 86

The Polyphonic Shree is a large band. Every year they recruit members for their World Tour. The Shree wants 9 musicians and twice as many singers as that. Last year, they had 15 singers and 10 musicians. How many more people do they want in the band this year?

Question 87

Jeffrey Sincomhoff has a ticket to the Polypohonic Shree concert. He is going to wrap himself in Christmas tree lights. He has 30 lights. It takes 5 size D batteries to light these lights. If there are more lights, they won't light with only 5 size D batteries. How many size D batteries does he need it he wants to wear a string of 42 lights?

Question 88

Yani and 2 other members of his team qualified for the International Cup Stacking Competition. The other members are Mallory, who is Yani's nemesis, and Lily, who is Mallory's best friend. Yani doesn't want Mallory to go because Mallory beats Yani at everything. Mallory tells Yani "If you can guess how many cups I have in my box on the first try, I won't go," she said. "I started with 8 red cups and 3 blue cups. I doubled the number of blue cups, added 4 red cups, and then took away from the red cups a number equal to the half the difference between the red cups and the blue cups. Take as long as you like. You can write numbers down if it helps, but no drawing pictures." Can you help Yani? You are not allowed to draw any pictures, but you can write numbers as you go.

Bonus Question: Suppose that Yani gets this problem correct on the first try. What is Mallory going to do?

Question 89

Mallory and Lily are playing the game called Zombie Slides and Steps. On her first turn, Mallory rolls a 5 and lands on a space marked "Pick a Zombie Card". On her first turn, Lily rolls a 3 and lands on a space marked "Pick 2 Zombie cards". If each Zombie card allows the card holder to move ahead at least 2 spaces, is Mallory ahead of Lily after the first turn?

Question 90

In Yani's 4th grade class, the teacher graded the math test from yesterday and gave the tests back to the students. The teacher announced to the class "If you get a problem correct, you didn't learn anything. If you got a problem wrong, then you learned something and you have become smarter." Yani got his test back. He missed 11 problems out of 30. Mallory got her math test back. She missed 4 word problems and 4 multiplication problems, but got the rest correct. How many more problems did Mallory get correct than Yani?

Bonus Question: Did Yani finally beat Mallory at something?

Question 91

The producer of the upcoming movie "Zoomies: The Return of the Zing" is looking for a child to play a roll. This roll requires singing the song "Roll of the Zombies". Neither Oliver nor Yani can sing well, but they both start practicing for the audition in 2 weeks. Yani practices the song 23 times the first week and 17 times the second week. Oliver practices the song 10 times each week. When they both try out, the producer thinks to himself "this kid Yani is _____ as good as the kid Oliver." What phrase did the producer use? The choices are "not", "almost", "twice", "three times", "four times".

Bonus Question: Yani and Oliver both had fun auditioning because they got to dress up as Zombies. Who got the part?

Question 92

There was a kid who practiced the song "Roll of the Zombies" 1000 times, and since he was better than everyone else, he got the part. He practices 200 times in the tub, 400 times in the shower, 300 times on the school bus, and the other times in his bedroom. How many fewer times did he practice while dry than while wet?

Bonus Question: Something bad would happen when he practiced sometimes. What was it?

Question 93

Yani packed for his trip to the International Cup Stacking Championships. He packed his bag with a tooth brush, some books, and 8 donuts and 8 cupcakes for snacks. His mom is not happy with his unhealthy snacks and told him to go to the garden and get 2 vegetables for every unhealthy snack he brings. Yani picked up a backpack and went to the garden. He likes carrots, and there are lots of carrots in the garden. He likes pickles even more and suddenly saw a jar of pickles. If Yani puts all 25 of the pickles from the jar in his backpack, how many carrots does he need to get?

Bonus Question: What did Yani forget to pack?

Super Bonus Question: What is wrong, odd, or interesting about this problem?

Question 94

Yani and Oliver are playing a game. Each player starts out with 10 mints and 10 raisins in a bowl. Each person gets to role a single dice (called a die) once. Whatever the number is, that person takes this number of skittles from the other player's bowl and then puts that number of raisins in the other player's bowl. Then both players have to eat what is in their bowl. Yani rolls the die and gets a 5. Oliver gets a 3. How many more raisins does Oliver have than Yani has raisins?

Bonus Question: Who won?

Question 95

Lily and Mallory were playing catch with a barrel cactus. After the game, Lily had 5 spines in her left hand and 12 spines in her right hand. Mallory had 7 spines in her left hand and 5 spines in her right hand. After each girl removed 8 spines, how many fewer spines did Mallory have in her hands than Lily?

Bonus Question: How many fewer spines did Mallory have in her hands than Lily before they each removed 8 spines?

Super Bonus Question: Why is this the same answer?

Super Duper Bonus Question: Which type of cactus has more spines, a barrel cactus or a saguaro cactus?

Question 96

Sumi Von Gusa left his magic wand at Oliver's house. Oliver tried out the wand on his fish. Oliver has 2 fish tanks in his house. One tank has 13 tiny guppies and the other tank has 12 minnows. He waved the wand at the guppy tank and 5 of them reappeared in the minnow tank. He waved the wand at the minnow tank, and 3 of the minnows turned into adult fish. How many more small fish are in the minnow tank than the guppy tank?

Question 97

Oliver was going to try the wand on the lamps next, but suddenly part of the tank with the guppies caught on fire. He called the fire department and when everyone arrived, he took them to the tank. A large fire truck showed up with 6 firemen, and a small fire truck showed up with 7 more fireman. Then a clown car showed up with clowns each holding a bucket of water. There were 21 people standing in front of the guppy tank. How many people were clowns?

Bonus Question: What was on fire? Be very specific.

Question 98

The fire house is next to the Clown Training Center. The fireman and the clowns had a contest to see who could fill up the most buckets in 5 minutes. At the end of 5 minutes, the clowns had a row of 7 filled buckets, and also a row of filled buckets stacked on top of that. The fireman had a row of 5 buckets, with 2 more rows of filled buckets stacked on top of the first row. Who won the contest?

You can draw a picture if you like.

Bonus Question: Why do you think the winners won?

Question 99

Right before the International Cup Stacking Competition, Yani's coach became very sick. Yani's mother asked Oliver's uncle if he would coach. Oliver's uncle told Yani's mother that he will do it if he can find 12 plastic cups in his house. Oliver's uncle has 14 complete place settings all made out of plastic on his long table, and 1 extra place setting in the cupboard that is missing a cup. Each place setting has 2 cups, a big one and a small one. While he was counting cups, his pet elephant sat on the table and crushed 5 place settings, and Oliver's uncle lost 1/3 of the rest of the cups in the mess. Is Oliver's uncle going to become the coach?

Bonus Question: If Yani's mother finds a plastic cup in her purse and gives it to Oliver's uncle, will he become the coach now?

Super Bonus Question: Who is Oliver's uncle?

Question 100

Yani and his team arrived at the cup stacking completions. It was on an island. The island has 900 stone statues on it. The average statue is 13 feet tall and weighs 13 tons. The biggest statue is 32 feet tall and weighs 96 tons. How much more does each foot of the big statue weigh than each foot of the small statue weigh? You can use a calculator if you write out all of the equations you solve first.

Bonus Question: What is the name of this island?

Super Bonus Question: How much does a ton weigh?

Section 2

Question 1

Example Question	Solution
$3 F = 7$	$F = \text{"} + 4 \text{"}$
$4 F = ?$	$4 + 4 = 8$

A. $F = 3 + 1$

$5 F = ?$

4	5	8	9
○	○	○	○

D. $4 F + 2 = 9$

$6 F = ?$

0	3	6	9
○	○	○	○

B. $4 + 5 = F$

$F + 3 = ?$

4	5	9	12
○	○	○	○

E. $F = 5 + 6$

$10 F = ?$

0	11	21	31
○	○	○	○

C. $10 F = 5$

$15 F = ?$

5	10	15	20
○	○	○	○

F. $F + 2 = 1 + 2$

$5 F F F = ?$

0	2	6	8
○	○	○	○

Question 2

Example Question	Solution
3 F = 7	F = "+ 4"
4 F = ?	4 + 4 = 8

A.   8 F = 11

     2 F = ?

  8   6   10   5
◯   ◯   ◯   ◯

D.   8 F = 13

     10 F = ?

  1   2   3   15
◯   ◯   ◯   ◯

B.   12 F = 19

     4 F = ?

  0   6   10   11
◯   ◯   ◯   ◯

E.   9 F = 5

     10 F = ?

  0   6   16   19
◯   ◯   ◯   ◯

C.   15 F = 9

     6 F = ?

  0   2   4   8
◯   ◯   ◯   ◯

F.   12 F = 3

     19 F = ?

  9   10   12   19
◯   ◯   ◯   ◯

Question 3

Example Question	Solution
3 F = 7	F = "+ 4"
4 F = ?	4 + 4 = 8

A. 5 F = 10

   3 F = ?

   4   6   10   5
   ○   ○   ○   ○

D. 12 F = 12

   10 F = ?

   2   10   22   23
   ○   ○   ○   ○

B. 7 F = 13

   13 F = ?

   0   6   7   19
   ○   ○   ○   ○

E. 12 F = 7

   9 F = ?

   0   3   4   14
   ○   ○   ○   ○

C. 16 F = 8

   8 F = ?

   1   2   4   8
   ○   ○   ○   ○

F. 11 F = 5

   7 F = ?

   0   1   2   5
   ○   ○   ○   ○

Question 4

A.　　9 F = 7

　　　17 F = ?

2	11	12	15
◯	◯	◯	◯

D.　　13 F − 5 = 3

　　　8 F = ?

0	3	5	10
◯	◯	◯	◯

B.　　6 F + 3 = 13

　　　10 F = ?

0	6	12	14
◯	◯	◯	◯

E.　　8 F = 18

　　　13 F − 7 = ?

6	14	16	33
◯	◯	◯	◯

C.　　14 F = 6

　　　11 F = ?

0	1	3	5
◯	◯	◯	◯

F.　　3 F = 12

　　　19 F − 1 = ?

9	10	11	27
◯	◯	◯	◯

Question 5

A.   14 F = 17

       12 F =   ?

    3   5   15   17
    ○   ○   ○   ○

D.   14 F = 7 + 2

       10 F = ? + 1

    4   5   6   7
    ○   ○   ○   ○

B.   12 F = 19

       4 F = ?

    7   8   11   12
    ○   ○   ○   ○

E.   15 F - 1 = 5

       10 F = ?

    1   3   9   10
    ○   ○   ○   ○

C.   15 F = 9

       6 F = ?

    0   5   6   9
    ○   ○   ○   ○

F.   7 F = 15

       19 − 8 F = ?

    3   7   9   19
    ○   ○   ○   ○

Question 6

A.　　4 F = 8

　　　8 F = ?

　11　　13　　15　　16
　◯　　◯　　◯　　◯

B.　　14 F = 21

　　　10 F = ?

　3　　16　　17　　30
　◯　　◯　　◯　　◯

C.　　4 F = 12

　　　F = ? + 2

　3　　5　　6　　7
　◯　　◯　　◯　　◯

D.　　8 F = 13

　　　20 = ? F

　10　　15　　20　　25
　◯　　◯　　◯　　◯

E.　　9 F = 5

　　　10 F = ?

　3　　5　　6　　14
　◯　　◯　　◯　　◯

F.　　12 F = 3

　　　16 F = ?

　4　　6　　8　　10
　◯　　◯　　◯　　◯

Question 7

A.
$$15\,f = 7$$
$$16\,f = ?$$

7	8	9	10
◯	◯	◯	◯

D.
$$4\,F + 1 = 13$$
$$12\,F = ?$$

4	6	18	20
◯	◯	◯	◯

B.
$$18\,B - 5 = 0$$
$$13\,B + 3 = ?$$

0	3	13	16
◯	◯	◯	◯

E.
$$13 = 2\,F - 3$$
$$16\,F = ?$$

0	2	14	30
◯	◯	◯	◯

C.
$$9 = F - 7$$
$$19 - ? = F$$

3	6	9	12
◯	◯	◯	◯

F.
$$5\,F + 6 = 18$$
$$9 = 1\,F + ?$$

0	1	2	5
◯	◯	◯	◯

Question 8

A.   5 F = 15

   20 F F = ?

   10   20   30   40
   ⬭   ⬭   ⬭   ⬭

B.   17 F = 11

   12 F F = ?

   0   6   18   24
   ⬭   ⬭   ⬭   ⬭

C.   9 F = 13

   4 F F = ?

   4   8   12   16
   ⬭   ⬭   ⬭   ⬭

D.   18 F = 15

   11 F F = ?

   3   5   7   8
   ⬭   ⬭   ⬭   ⬭

E.   19 F = 9

   30 F F = ?

   9   10   12   20
   ⬭   ⬭   ⬭   ⬭

F.   9 F = 17

   0 F F F = ?

   16   18   24   30
   ⬭   ⬭   ⬭   ⬭

Question 9

A. $4 + F = 2 + 11$

       $5 + F - 3 = ?$

10	11	12	13
◯	◯	◯	◯

D. $7 F + 3 = 5 + 5$

       $8 - ? = F + 3 + 5$

0	1	4	5
◯	◯	◯	◯

B. $15 F + 3 = 6$

       $5 + 20 F = ?$

0	6	9	24
◯	◯	◯	◯

E. $13 F = 10 - 3$

       $9 + 4 = ? F$

6	7	16	19
◯	◯	◯	◯

C. $F + 7 = 16 - 15$

       $13 F F = 15 - ?$

0	1	14	15
◯	◯	◯	◯

F. $5 F F = 16 - 3$

       $9 F - 3 = 4 F F - ?$

0	2	4	6
◯	◯	◯	◯

Question 10

A. $9 + 7\ F = 5 + 9$

         $10\ F\ F = 9 + 4 - ?$

3	7	9	10
◯	◯	◯	◯

D. $15 - 6 = 3\ F$

         $2\ F\ F = 9 + ?$

0	3	6	9
◯	◯	◯	◯

B. $16 - 9 = F + 3$

         $4\ F\ F + 4 = 4 \times 4 + ?$

0	4	8	16
◯	◯	◯	◯

E. $3 + 6 - 5 = 7\ F - 8$

         $5\ F + 5 = 7 + ?$

4	5	6	8
◯	◯	◯	◯

C. $5 + 12\ F = 9 + 8$

         $3\ F + 8 = 4 + ?$

0	4	7	8
◯	◯	◯	◯

F. $13 - 9 = 5 + 5\ F$

         $18\ F - 5 = 16 - ?$

5	7	9	11
◯	◯	◯	◯

Question 11

A. $F + 19 = 38 - 18$

1 $F + 7 = 4 + 5 + ?$

0	5	9	10
⬭	⬭	⬭	⬭

D. $12\ F + 7 = 15 - 4$

$16\ F + 3 = ? + 6$

0	2	4	5
⬭	⬭	⬭	⬭

B. $5\ F - 8 = 7 + 5$

$3\ F + 3 = 8 + ?$

0	3	4	7
⬭	⬭	⬭	⬭

E. $23\ F + 2 = 16 \div 2$

$17\ F + 9 = 13 - 7 + ?$

0	1	2	3
⬭	⬭	⬭	⬭

C. $9\ F = 44 + 55$

$33 + 77 - ? = 10\ F$

10	15	110	120
⬭	⬭	⬭	⬭

F. $F + 20 = 14 + 16$

$15\ F - 9 = 9 + 7 - ?$

0	7	9	10
⬭	⬭	⬭	⬭

Question 12

The symbol $\not{F}$ means "not F". So if F = " + 3 ", then $\not{F}$ = " – 3".

A.
12 F + 3 = 2 x 10

15 $\not{F}$ - 3 = 10 - ?

0	3	7	11
◯	◯	◯	◯

D.
20 F F = 2 × 3

9 $\not{F}$ - 7 = 29 - ?

0	7	13	20
◯	◯	◯	◯

B.
18 $\not{F}$ = 18 – 9

3 F + 6 F = 6 + ?

2	6	8	12
◯	◯	◯	◯

E.
17 F – 8 = 15 – 10

8 F $\not{F}$ $\not{F}$ = 7 + ?

0	4	5	9
◯	◯	◯	◯

C.
3 F + 7 = 11 + 12

2 F - ? = 16 – 9

8	9	10	11
◯	◯	◯	◯

F.
F + 20 = 14 + 16

15 F – 9 = 9 + 7 - ?

0	7	9	10
◯	◯	◯	◯

Question 13

A.
$$19\,F = 9 + 3$$
$$9 + ? = 20\,F$$

4	7	11	14
○	○	○	○

D.
$$14\,F = 16 \div 2$$
$$4 + 4\,F = 29 - ?$$

2	4	6	27
○	○	○	○

B.
$$6 + 7\,F = 9 - 4$$
$$12 + 7\,F = 11 - ?$$

0	11	15	23
○	○	○	○

E.
$$20 - 0\,F = 9 + 4$$
$$16 - ? = 21\,F\,F$$

9	10	12	20
○	○	○	○

C.
$$5 + 2\,F = 15 - 4$$
$$6 + 9 = 3\,F + ?$$

4	6	7	9
○	○	○	○

F.
$$25\,F - 3 = 15 \div 3$$
$$6 \times 0 = 23\,F - ?$$

0	1	3	6
○	○	○	○

Question 14

A.   4 F = 11

         8 G = 11

         5 F G = ?

3	5	15	17
⬭	⬭	⬭	⬭

D.   19 G = 9

         5 F = 0

         15 F G = ?

0	1	2	3
⬭	⬭	⬭	⬭

B.   1 F = 16

         11 G = 3

         20 F G = ?

5	12	13	27
⬭	⬭	⬭	⬭

E.   40 F = 30

         14 G = 9

         15 F G = ?

0	15	25	30
⬭	⬭	⬭	⬭

C.   27 F = 29

         29 G = 27

         256 F G = ?

252	254	256	258
⬭	⬭	⬭	⬭

F.   17 F = 6

         17 G = 15

         17 F G = ?

2	4	6	15
⬭	⬭	⬭	⬭

Question 15

A.   18 F = 12

         22 G = 29

         9 F G = ?

3	10	16	27
◯	◯	◯	◯

B.   12 F + 3 = 6

         11 G = 5

         17 F G = ?

0	1	2	3
◯	◯	◯	◯

C.   7 F = 16

         8 G + 4 = 17

         1 F G = ?

1	5	9	15
◯	◯	◯	◯

D.   7 F + 1 = 15

         11 g = 4

         12 F g = ?

-2	5	12	17
◯	◯	◯	◯

E.   16 F − 4 = 3

         3 G = 9

         5 G F = ?

0	2	4	6
◯	◯	◯	◯

F.   7 F F = 11

         19 G G = 11

         8 F G = ?

5	6	12	13
◯	◯	◯	◯

Question 16

A.

$13 + 7 = F + 5$

$11 - 8 = 18 - 3 G$

$F + 2 G = 12 - 6 - ?$

0	3	5	15
◯	◯	◯	◯

D.

$1 F + 13 = 12 \times 2$

$13 G = 29 + 7$

$5 G - ? = 2 F - 0$

10	16	23	39
◯	◯	◯	◯

B.

$12 G + 4 = 4 + 8$

$8 F G = 4 + 8$

$11 F + 5 = 27 - ?$

0	3	6	9
◯	◯	◯	◯

E.

$7 F + 3 = 13 - 9$

$4 + 4 = 15 G - 13$

$9 F + 15 = 21 G - ?$

9	10	12	20
◯	◯	◯	◯

C.

$2 F + 2 = 21 - 9$

$2 G + 1 = 16 - 6$

$8 F = 3 G + ?$

2	6	8	30
◯	◯	◯	◯

F.

$50 F + 3 = 6 + 7$

$40 + 50 = 99 G$

$50 F + 3 = 14 G + ?$

0	4	8	10
◯	◯	◯	◯

Question 17

A.
$3 + F = 19 - 7$

$18\ G\ G = 4 + 4$

$8\ F = 18\ G + ?$

0	1	3	4
◯	◯	◯	◯

D.
$14\ F - 7 = 19 - 14$

$9 - 7 = 16\ G - 1$

$17 - ? - 3 = 20\ F\ G$

2	11	13	15
◯	◯	◯	◯

B.
$7 + 7 = 5 + 17\ F$

$19 - 4 = 7 + 8\ G$

$10\ F + 2 = 12\ G - ?$

0	8	10	12
◯	◯	◯	◯

E.
$10\ F + 10 = 11 - 7$

$20\ F + 6 = 5\ G + 1$

$20\ F\ G = 14 - 6 - ?$

0	2	5	12
◯	◯	◯	◯

C.
$F + 3 = 17 - 7$

$6 + 6 = 5\ G - 5$

$9\ F + 9 = 6\ G + ?$

0	12	14	19
◯	◯	◯	◯

F.
$5\ F + 3 = 7 + 7$

$10\ G - 5 = 10 \div 2$

$5\ F\ G = 15 - ?$

3	4	9	19
◯	◯	◯	◯

Question 18

The symbol $\mathfrak{F}$ means "not F". So if F = " + 3 ", then $\mathfrak{F}$ = " − 3".

A.   15 F = 8

    5 G = 12

    14 F $\mathfrak{G}$ = ?

0	7	14	21
◯	◯	◯	◯

D.   6 F = 13

    6 G G = 12

    10 F $\mathfrak{F}$ $\mathfrak{G}$ = ?

0	3	7	10
◯	◯	◯	◯

B.   18 F = 11

    19 G = 11

    5 $\mathfrak{F}$ $\mathfrak{G}$ = ?

0	12	13	20
◯	◯	◯	◯

E.   9 F F = 15

    13 G = 3

    8 $\mathfrak{F}$ $\mathfrak{G}$ = ?

3	10	15	18
◯	◯	◯	◯

C.   4 G = 9

    15 F = 9

    17 $\mathfrak{F}$ G = ?

0	6	9	28
◯	◯	◯	◯

F.   20 F F = 8

    4 G G = 12

    7 $\mathfrak{F}$ G = ?

0	5	6	9
◯	◯	◯	◯

Question 19

A.   13 F + 5 = 22

12 G = 6

0 𝔉 𝔊 = ?

0	1	2	3
⬭	⬭	⬭	⬭

D.   13 F + 3 = 10

12 𝔊 = 6

𝔉 G = ?

0	6	12	18
⬭	⬭	⬭	⬭

B.   1 + 15 F = 9

18 𝔊 − 3 = 10

11 𝔊 𝔉 = ?

5	8	10	13
⬭	⬭	⬭	⬭

E.   14 = F + 8

G + 4 = 3 + 10

19 𝔉 + G = ?

9	12	22	25
⬭	⬭	⬭	⬭

C.   3 𝔉 + 7 = 12

6 𝔊 = 10

3 F + 4 G = ?

0	1	4	6
⬭	⬭	⬭	⬭

F.   𝔉 = 18 + F + F

14 𝔊 = 8

6 F G = ?

0	3	6	9
⬭	⬭	⬭	⬭

Question 20

A.
$$5 = 18 \; 𝔉 - 3$$
$$𝔊 + 2 = 9 + 5$$
$$14 \; 𝔉 = ? + G$$

0   5   12   16
◯   ◯   ◯   ◯

D.
$$17 \; F - 6 = 11 - 7$$
$$13 + 5 = 16 \; 𝔊 + 8$$
$$𝔉 + 3 = 25 - ?$$

0   8   12   18
◯   ◯   ◯   ◯

B.
$$7 + 𝔉 = 10 - 3$$
$$6 + 3 = 19 \; G$$
$$7 + F \; 𝔊 = 17 - ?$$

0   10   17   23
◯   ◯   ◯   ◯

E.
$$7 \; F + 3 = 25 - 3$$
$$20 \; 𝔊 \; 𝔊 = 16$$
$$25 \; 𝔉 \; G = 5 + ?$$

9   10   22   25
◯   ◯   ◯   ◯

C.
$$15 \; 𝔉 + 3 = 23$$
$$15 \; G - 4 = 4 \times 2$$
$$12 \; 𝔉 \; 𝔊 = ?$$

3   5   20   22
◯   ◯   ◯   ◯

F.
$$17 - 5 \; G = 22$$
$$10 + 13 = 𝔉 + 6$$
$$𝔉 - 9 = 20 \; 𝔊 - ?$$

2   10   12   14
◯   ◯   ◯   ◯

Solutions

Section 1

Question 1

Oliver put 10 + 4 = 14 candles on the cake. Hannah is only 3, so her mom had to take 14 − 3 = 11 candles off of the cake.

This is a marginally convoluted problem, at the beginner's level, that introduces 2 of the supporting characters of this workbook. These children are not the normal boring children found in most workbooks. When Hannah's mom asked Oliver to put the candles on the cake, he wanted to do something special for Hannah because a birthday is special. He blew it.

The slightly convoluted nature of these problems is introducing the skills of "read it again" and "try again because you forgot something". As a math coach and parent, your job is to encourage your child to read the problem again, not to explain it.

Question 2

There are 9 + 6 = 15 hats in the box. Hannah took 6 + 8 = 14 hats. Oliver will find 15 − 14 = 1 hat left. From that point, you can argue whether the hat is green or pink. My son made a good case for green because pink hats belong on dolls and green hats on stuffed animals. I say Oliver ended up with a pink hat because younger siblings tend to affect outcomes that are undesirable.

Remember that the two primary goals of this book are to teach the child to spend lots of time with the question and to teach the child that getting the answer wrong 5 times is not a big deal.

Question 3

This is very easy math but it is very hard to figure out what this problem is asking. If your child doesn't get it after 5 re-readings of the question, ask your child to read it out loud and explain it to you. Feign bafflement.

She took 8 − 5 = 3 hats off of the stuffed animals. Therefore 6 − 5 = 1 dolls are wearing hats and 3 stuffed animals are wearing hats. 3 + 1 = 4 stuffed animals and dolls are wearing hats.

Question 4

The pants has 8 legs and the sweater has 8 arms. This is true in all of the cartoons and costumes I've seen. I've never seen an octopus wearing both pants and a sweater. The point of this question is to take 20 minutes to figure out how many arms an octopus sweater has (8) and how many legs octopus pants have (8).

Since Oliver only has 2 arms and 2 legs, there are 8 + 8 − 2 − 2 = 12 sweater arms and pant legs with no leg or arm in them.

Even my 11 year old had trouble coming to terms with octopus pants and sweaters.

Bonus Question: I really have no idea. Hopefully your child can come up with something. I get lots of goofy answers to the bonus questions which demonstrate that thinking is going on, but I don't always get realistic, common sense answers. You'll find out why he had these costumes in question 83 (approximately).

Question 5

This question is an introductory level question on letting your child think. Most parents never let their children think. That's why only 5% of the population qualifies for accelerated or gifted programs. More on this later.

First, you have to wait until your child figures out that we don't know how many slices have seeds, because we don't know how many seeds are in this apple. That could take a long time because a child would never imagine a math workbook has a question that requires thinking. Then you have to follow these steps. This is the most important part of the question – you following these steps:

Say "I don't know," which you don't. Some of you think you do but you really don't. My son argued that there were 4 seeds. I tried to lecture him on the scientific method, but when I cut an apple open, in front of him, there were 4 seeds so I lost all credibility.

Instead of grabbing an apple like I did, ask "How are **you** going to figure out how many seeds are in this apple?"

If your child gets almost no exercise because his day is filled with piano, reading, homework, and editing his father's math workbooks, then you have lots of apples around the house for obvious reasons so your child might cut one up. My fallback plan is "look it up on the internet". If your child doesn't suggest anything, than this question is going to take a few days and you just have to wait. By the way, you might ask how many seeds are in an orange while you are doing research. I love distractions during math because it requires the child to come back to the question and read it again, which is one of the Big Five skills.

The whole purpose of this question is for your child to come up with the equation and solve it. If you find that an apple has 5 seeds, the answer is $5 - 2 = 3$, but you might find that the number of seeds is 4 or another number.

Question 6

In case you blew it in question 6, here's another question that requires your child to figure out that there is a value missing from the question and she has to figure it out or look it up for herself.

There are 9 justices on the court, and $9 - 6 = 3$ do not get a frosted donut and are therefore not happy. Technically, one or more justices could have grabbed multiple frosted donuts, but that is beyond the level in this workbook.

Bonus Question: You may have to ask your child which donuts the clerk ate. This question is an eye opener. If he ate 2 frosted donuts, $9 - 4 = 5$ justices are not happy and they will get a new clerk, the clerk will not be happy either. If the clerk ate 1 frosted donut, then $9 - 5 = 4$ justices are not happy. If the clerk at 2 unfrosted donuts, then the answer does not change.

Super Bonus Question: There are $12 - 9 = 3$ donuts left. There are 3 unhappy justices because each one got a single unfrosted donut. The clerk can give each of these 3 justices a second donut.

The Super Bonus Question is almost a brain teaser but not quite. My children and I did done a lot of brain teasers as part of the research leading up to this workbook. I like brain teasers because they requires thinking about a question for a long, long time, but I don't like them because it is usually impossible to derive the answer from the question which undermines the figuring out process. The answer usually depends on some obscure fact that the children don't know, like "hard boiled eggs float". This book has very few questions resembling brain teasers until question 94 which you'll probably never get to. Somewhere around question 60 or 80, most parents have solidly learned the skills that I want to teach, and as a bonus, so have the children.

In this case, I was thinking "give the 3 unhappy justices 2 donuts each" but my sons argued "frost the donuts himself" and won the argument.

Question 7

Hannah has 5 roses with petals. If your child counts by 5's, there are 25 rose petals. Since we don't know how many petals are on the daisy, it could be as small as 21, in which case she would have more rose petals, and as large as 34, in which case she does not have more rose petals. I feel like I'm spoon feeding the child with this easy problem, but a problem like this takes a long time to understand for a beginning brainiac. The answer is that we don't know. "Probably" is a good answer for partial credit.

Ideally your child would say "no" or "I don't know", and you could argue that the answer is yes and subsequently lose the argument. You might try being wrong on adding or subtracting problems and make a big show of trying to figure out the problem a second or third time on your own before you determine that yes, in fact your child is correct. The point isn't to raise argumentative children but to demonstrate that getting an incorrect answer and having to solve the problem or reread the problem a few more times is a normal part of math, even for an adult. After that, your children will have a brand new attitude toward homework – an attitude that is the opposite of frustration.

Bonus Question: Rose petals are not poisonous, but every single person in my neighborhood dumps tons of pesticides on they lawns and gardens, so anything that grows outdoors is probably covered with dangerous chemicals. If there are no dangerous chemicals on the rose, then there are probably tiny little bugs that I don't want to eat.

Super Bonus Question: Pickles are cucumbers that are processed after they are picked. You can explore processing on your own. It would be completely ridiculous and absurd to have pickles in a garden and only an insane math workbook writer would even consider such a ludicrous idea. If you see a math workbook with pickles in a garden, you should throw it away immediately.

Question 8

Mantes is the plural of mantis. Instead of telling this to your child, you should just look it up on the internet on google images. There you will find a few pictures of a mantis and lots of pictures of buildings. Obviously, Mallory is not going to make paper cathedrals.

We're in the easy zone right now. Practice letting your child read and reread the question and figure out what it is asking with little to no help from you, other than saying "Read it again."

Mallory needs to make 200 – 100 – 50 = 50 more. You as the parent don't really care about the answer. Whether your child got it right or not, do not tell the answer but ask your child how many mantes her friends made. The answer is 150. Ask your child how to figure out how many Mallory needs to make if her friends made 150. The answer is 200 – 150 = 50. You can also get this answer by subtracting 100 from 200 and then subtracting 100 from 50.

The reason we are going to all this trouble is because we are enforcing best practices for academic coaching and teaching math:

1. You don't care about right or wrong answers.

2. You are more concerned with understanding the problem, picking it a part, and looking at it from various perspectives regardless of what the solution is.

Bonus Question: Mallory needs at least 50 x 2 = 100 pieces of paper. The question that your child is probably going to miss is this: Do Yani and Lily need Mallory to give them paper or will they get their own paper? 400 is a good answer.

Apologies to Yannis for misspelling his name throughout this book.

Question 9

This is a fun problem to think about if you like math. It involves visualization and not as much working memory. This would be a good question to think about over the next 6 weeks or so. Feel free not to share the answer with your child.

The answer is one child should get the first and the forth box, and the other child should get the other 2.

Bonus Question: if all 3 boxes can fit in the 4ᵗʰ box without being encapsulated, because they are filled with pom poms, then one child should get the 4ᵗʰ box, and the other child should get the other 3.

Super Bonus Question: Mallory is giving Yani and Lily the pom poms to decorate the paper mantes from question 8.

At this point, it's worth mentioning that if your child is getting all of these problems wrong, the child is learning the skills that this book is teaching.

Question 10

Yani's total score was $5 + 6 + 9 = 20$. Mallory needs at least a $21 - 8 - 4 = 9$ from Bowen. Mallory received either a 9 or a 10 from Bowen. Since there is no limit on the scores, she could also receive an 11, 12, 13, or higher. Bowen could have given Mallory a 103, which is totally silly and makes math much more fun.

Question 11

Oliver threw the Frisbee $9 + 6$ yards $= 15$ yards. Kai threw the Frisbee $7 + 12 = 19$ yards. We can safely assume that Oliver and Kai are throwing the Frisbees in a straight line toward the hole, because without this assumption, we need trigonometry, but I'll save that for Test Prep Math Level 15.

Bonus Question: Kai is closer. Kai is $19 - 15 = 4$ yards closer.

If you want to change the pace of math in your house, ask how close to the hole they are. The answer is $30 - 15 = 15$ yards for Oliver and $30 - 19 = 11$ yards for Kai. Now how much closer is Kai? $15 - 11 = 4$ yards. Don't forget to get things wrong occasionally when you are figuring out the answer to check your child's solution. Did your child get the same solution solving the problem backwards?

Question 12

The red lipped batfish now has 3 + 4 = 7 lipsticks, so she needs 7 – 5 = 2 more shells. Feel free to look up the red lipped batfish on the internet.

Ideally, you live in a house where every day you are coming across interesting questions like what is a bat fish or how many seeds are in an apple and then doing a little research and learning something new. I wish our house was like this so I could raise two scientists. We didn't start doing this formally until I started writing these questions.

Question 13

It will probably take 2 x 7 = 14 minutes to comb the hair of the second cat, and both cats will therefore take 7 + 14 = 21 minutes.

The question is vague on how long it takes to groom the second cat. Hopefully you didn't point out to your child that it takes 2 x 7. If you did, stop it. If your child is totally baffled, get 2 empty measuring cups, one twice as big as the other. Ask your child to find out how long it takes to fill each cup.

Question 14

This problem is in the spirit of Common Core. The short answer is "The square has more room for pennies". If your child answers this immediately make them explain further. No one learns anything from getting a problem correct.

Solving this problem requires a discussion of what "same size" means for a circle and a square. A circle is characterized by diameter, and a square is characterized by width, so I'm going to say that the diameter equals the width. You could argue "area", in which case the answer should be the same number of pennies.

If the circle fits within the square, and the square has extra corners to place pennies, then the square can fit more pennies.

If you get blank looks, help your child draw a 7 inch square on one piece of paper and a 7 inch circle on another, of find something round about 6 or 7 inches to use as a template and draw a square the same size. Ask for an explanation. Then draw the two shapes so that the circle is inscribed in the square. Define the term "inscribed".

Question 15

Hannah has 8 + 13 = 21 pennies. The answer is 2 nickels, a dime, and a penny. The only way I know how to solve this problem is to draw a bunch of coins and then find which combination adds up to 21.

I used to hate questions like this as a child. How could this possibly be math? I thought that math was mastering and applying math concepts and formulas. I added this problem to the book for 2 reasons. First, this workbook is teaching patience. The child and parent have to approach math problems expecting to spend a long time trying to figure them out or school will be very challenging in later grades. Secondly, this work book is teaching problem solving and trying different options is a key problem solving technique. Once a parent knows these techniques, helping with math homework is far less taxing.

Question 16

The mouse has 20 pieces of cheese. The mouse has 20 − 5 x 2 = 10 pieces left after sharing with the cat, and 10 − 5 = 5 pieces left after eating 5 pieces.

Bonus Question: The problem is that even a cat who eats cheese has to drink and go to the bathroom. There may be other problems as well that I didn't think of.

Question 17

Like many problems, this problem is an exercise in understanding what the question is asking, and then understanding the question enough to draw a picture to be solved. The math is fairly complicated algebra, but the picture is a fairly simple problem to solve. I shouldn't use the word "simple" because it will probably take a long time to get the correct answer.

You may want to save this problem for later or try again every 2 weeks or so. This is a very important problem but it also belongs at about #85 in difficulty. I put this one here intentionally.

First, you may want to hand your child a calendar or have them draw one. The main challenge for the child is to label the days with 0, 1, or 2 matches used while they come to terms with the question. This is the primary challenge. After that, reread the question again and start counting the days.

My diagram looks like this: 2 0 1 0 2 0 1 … where each number represents the number of matches used each day. If we count today in the answer, the answer is 41 days.

Bonus Question: Changing the diagram to 1 0 2 0 1 0 2 …, and counting, it takes 43 days. Therefore it takes 43 − 41 = 2 days.

Of course, when I say half the time it takes 1 match and half the time it takes 2 matches, you could argue through probability theory that they light the fire with 2 matches every time, but then I would ask for the full solution set and you'd be working on this problem a long time.

Super Bonus Question: A normal human would answer either 0, 1, or 2. A mathematician would answer 3 matches every 4 days. A way to rephrase this question is: what is the pattern of usages, as in what is the pattern. If your child is going to face a GAT test in the next year, do not skip this problem, don't short cut it, and spend a lot of time on it. There is a whole number pattern section on the test, and this question is like graduate school for number patterns.

For the Super Bonus Question, I'm looking for analysis of the pattern, not an answer suitable for graduate school. In other words, I'm not expecting a final answer, just thinking and talking.

Question 18

January has 31 days, so he ate 31 x 3 = 93 meals on this island. If he had 80 burritos, then he had to each coconuts for 93 − 80 meals = 13 coconuts, assuming 1 per meal.

Bonus Question: If he ate 13 coconuts, and only did so after the burritos were eaten, then he ate coconuts on 5 days. On 4 of these days, he ate coconuts for 4 x 3 = 12 meals, and on the fifth day, it was 1 coconut and 2 burritos.

Question 19

If you have 4 smaller earthworms, and they all continue to grow, they will each reach 10 feet and you will have 40 feet of earth worms.

The first problem with this question is that the slightly above average child will read this question and have no idea what it means.   Your child will probably ask you to explain this question to them, because no one ever lets the child figure things out for themselves, which is the single biggest skill they need in school and on GAT tests and in school. If you are prepared to let the child read it many times, draw pictures, try easier versions of the problem, and make mistakes, then you are prepared to help your child pick up advanced skills to put them in the 99th percentile.

Bonus Question: The second problem with this question is that if you cut a Giant Gippsland earthworm in half, it will die.   If you search on the internet for "what happens if you cut an earthworm in half", you'll find out that it will either die or the piece with the head might grow a tail.

So, if you are lucky, you'll only get 10 feet of one live earthworm and 7.5 feet of dead earthworm, but Giant Gippsland earthworms are fragile so you'll just end up with a dead earthworm in 4 pieces, 4 x 2.5 = 10 feet of dead earthworm.

This is the typical math question, and by "math", I mean "real math". Real math is a little bit of calculation, a lot of thinking, and mistrust of math questions in general because mostly they lead to zero or nonsense. In school, every single math question, like 3 + 7 = ? has an answer, and one and only one answer. School curriculum produces kids who don't think and hate math because 3 + 7 = ? becomes boring really fast.

While editing these workbooks, my kids came across a lot of question like this. "Dad, this question is totally wrong." Oops! Did I make another mistake? Their grades shot up in school. I don't think I made a mistake. 99% on the annual standardized test is not a mistake. We switched from 30 problems a day from regular workbooks to one goofy wrong question a day and experienced a thinking explosion. My youngest son gets one of these problems wrong each day, maybe wrong 3 or 4 times before he gets the right answer, and his accuracy rate in school increased tremendously. My older son just explains to me why the question is wrong.

Question 20

As equal as possible means dividing up the crackers and the cheese so that a kabob has either 4 or 5 pieces of cheese and 4 or 5 crackers. Only one kabob has 4 crackers, so at least one kabob has to have 5 crackers and 5 pieces of cheese. One kabob has either 4 pieces of cheese and 4 crackers or 5 pieces of cheese and 5 crackers, depending on how "equal" is defined, so the answer is 10 − 9 = 1 or 10 − 8 = 2.

If a child is struggling, makes mistakes, and takes more than 25 minutes, I will accept any reasonable answer confident that this workbook will increase their skill set. Then I'll help, even though I've told you repeatedly not to. The goal should be to help less and less.

If a child gets a correct answer in less than 5 minutes, I respond with "are there any other answers" followed by "which is the best answer"? Take that, overly bright child.

Bonus Question: The answer is 4. Furthermore, this question is nonsensical. My kids insisted that I keep this question in here to make up for all of the ones that are designed to elicit incorrect answers. On the internet, find the joke with the punchline "purple because aliens don't wear hats".

Question 21

Oliver has 4 x 8 = 32 slices of cheese. If he divides the crackers equally among the boxes, then he is going to use 40 crackers, because if he uses 32 crackers, he can get 1 more cracker in each box and he doesn't have 48. He has 40 – 32 = 8 more crackers in the boxes.

Bonus Question: First, depending on the state he's in, Oliver will need to register with the state and get a health and sanitation license to produce food. His kitchen will be inspected. Then he needs a production plan and a marketing plan, not to mention a market analysis to determine potential sales. He may have to pay for shelf space.   Will he sell the Cheese and Cracker Kabobs to the grocery store on industry terms or on consignment? Will he create a store display? Most likely, the grocery store manager will note the likelihood that the first kid who eats a Kabob will choke on the stick and sue both the grocery store and Oliver's parents, so the grocery store will ask Oliver how big is his class action lawsuit fund. If the store manager has an IT background, he'll ask whether or not Oliver tested the UPC symbol against industry standard scanners.

For the purposes of this book, it's enough that the child wonders what the grocery manager is thinking and how a grocery store works. Just wondering is a leap. Math is full of wondering. I don't expect an answer at all to the bonus question, but when I mention some of the issues, lots of thinking takes place. My son's response was "how did you draw the UPC code?"

Question 22

The small fire truck went out 6 + 7 = 13 calls. The big truck went out 3 times. The small truck made 13 - 3 = 10 more calls than the fire truck.

Chicago consolidated 6 fire stations into one and built the new building at the end of my block. I hear sirens about every 45 minutes.

Bonus Question: This is a simple reading comprehension question complicated by the fact that there is a math problem in between the question and the part of the passage with the answer. The answer is "Oliver can hear the sirens". A better answer is "he can hear the sirens and each truck makes a different sound." An even better answer is just to circle the second sentence in the question and draw and arrow to the bonus question, but alas, my kids never do this.

Question 23

There are 8 – 3 – 1 = 4 big cushions left on the couch. There are 7 – 4 = 3 small cushions left on the couch. There are 4 – 3 = 1 more big cushion than small cushions left on the couch.

This question introduces the full working memory mode with really small integers.

My son came up with 2 models that used more than 4 couch cushions. I guess that's good. I made him draw pictures and asked questions about the structural integrity, and finally we had to go down to the basement couch to experiment.

Bonus Question: Hannah is left with a pile of 8 cushions on the floor. I have a hard time getting my kids to understand that an answer in a math workbook needs a number (usually, at least with a normal math workbook), but they keep saying "A pile of cushions". "I need a number with your answer, so find something with a number and put it in your answer". They are not always successful. Sometimes, I just get a blank look. To get from "blank look" to the number 8 is worth the 30 minutes this bonus question might take.

Question 24

Mallory's brother and sister's team score 1 + 4 = 5 runs in the first inning and 2 + 6 = 8 times in the second inning, for a total of 5 + 8 = 13. The other team scored 7 + 6 = 13 times. Mallory answered that the game was a tie.

I used to think that the best way to learn math is through games, sports, and puzzles. Silly contrived word problems are getting a bad rap in math education research and there is a movement to remove these from math curriculum. I agree to a point, and that point is at about the 75th percentile. After that, I love ridiculous convoluted word problems to get to 99 percent.

Question 25

Before you provide any guidance, let your child guess. A correct guess would be 20 − 3 − 8 = 9 unaccounted for members of the drift.

The first problem is to figure out that the word "drift" is in this sentence, and the second problem is to figure out what it means. It means baby pigs. A little internet searching will uncover hundreds of obscure words for groups of animals.

A truly gifted and talented child would get the answer without knowing the definition drift. For the rest of our children, they're never going to get these skills without being put in situations where the skills are required. Here it is.

For those of you who are wondering, when I say "truly gifted and talented" I mean one who mastered and applies problem solving skills and enjoys it so much that he stops doing other things.

Question 26

The elephants ate 5 + 7 = 12 peanuts, and the monkeys ate 5 + 9 = 14 bananas. There were 14 - 12 = 2 more bananas eaten than peanuts.

If your child is just learning arithmetic, I would prefer that your child sits there for 25 minutes trying to do this question in her brain, even if it takes 5 attempts to get the correct answer. You can use written equations or pictures if you like to help her formulate a mental model. I normally give up after 2 wrong answers and ask for a picture. The goal of this book, however, is building those parts of the brain that can solve a problem like this mentally.

If your child works independently and writes things down and draws pictures instead of solving each problem mentally, then they are about 8 years ahead in terms of skills so don't worry about it.

On this particular question, my son stated that the question doesn't say who ate the bananas and who ate the peanuts. It was a teaching moment. "Read the question again" I said.

Question 27

This question requires a picture. Yani sits in the middle at the end opposite his parents.

Bonus Question: Yani doesn't know if he likes peas or not because he never gets any.

Question 28

Yani and Mallory have 11 - 8 = 3 buckets left. Oliver and Lily have 18 - 13 = 5 buckets left. Oliver and Lily win.

It's not 100% clear to me who is on what team. I'm willing to bet that not many kids ask "who's on each team?" You can respond "I don't know. You tell me." The final answer will may vary. My son didn't ask, so I asked him.

Bonus Question: The only two places I can think of are the parking lot of a movie theater that made way too many buckets of popcorn and put them next to the dumpster and a research facility for a popcorn making company. "One of their houses" is not a likely answer, unless it's the house of Sumi Von Gusa where anything can happen.

Question 29

When Yani's mom is finished planting, there will be 30 - 24 = 6 spots left. Yani will use 12 - 6 = 6 pea seeds and there will be 6 pea seeds left over.

Question 30

She needs to make 9 x 2 = 18 eyebrows. With 5 pieces of felt, she can make 5 x 3 = 15 eyebrows. That means she will be short 18 – 15 = 3 eyebrows, which means that one mouse will have no eyebrows and one mouse will only have 1 eyebrow. Equivalently, with 15 eyebrows, she can make eyebrows for 7 mice, leaving 9 − 7 = 2 without a complete set.

This problem might need a picture to solve. What I like the most about this question, other than the fact that it involves felt eyebrows on toy mice, is that the answer isn't all that satisfying.

If your child draws a picture with the felt, the eyebrows on the felt, and the mice, with circles and arrows matching eyebrows with mice, the problem is solvable. This is the official best practices way to solve this problem. I prefer my kids to build mental models, get it wrong a few times, and keep trying until they get it correct. I'm looking at all of the curriculum between 4th and 8th grade when I say this.

Question 31

Oliver has $3,000,000 - $400 = $2,999,600 to pay 100 workers. Each worker gets $29,996. This is obviously a calculator question, but remember to take a lot of time to understand the problem before the calculator comes out.

Bonus Question: Hannah can buy $29,996/400 = 74.99 PS4's. There's no such thing as .99 of a PS4, so the answer is 74.

Super Bonus Question: There are 4 people who fair might apply to.

- $29,996 per worker is not a lot of money to live on, so his parents were being realistic. This is as fair as they can be, which may not be fair.

- Oliver gets a PS4 which is not a lot of money for coming up with a brainstorm idea, but life isn't always fair.

- The parents will have less trouble with Oliver playing a PS4 then Oliver spending all of his time in the high tech arcade he was planning to build with his earnings, so it's fair to them.

- Hannah got almost $30,000 for putting together 17 boxes of Cheese and Cracker Kabobs. The term "fair" really doesn't work here.

Question 32

He spent (100 x $2 = $200) + (.25 x 200 = $50) + $30 = $280. He will sell 200 packages at $3 and earn $600. He could make $600 - $280 = $320. So in theory, he would make money.

This is a totally inappropriate question for this age group unless you want them to think a lot and learn something new.

Bonus Question: Make sure the UPC code appears on the package or make the child read the question again or argue that the UPC code is on the back. Is the British flag in the bottom right? I don't know, the problem is not clear.

Super Bonus Question: You could buy a bag of Swedish fish for $2, or you could buy a bag of British Salmon that has only half of the candies for $3. You would not buy a bag of British Salmon because it is ridiculously expensive. Someone who is not good at math will buy British Salmon Candy.

Question 33

Which movie they can afford to go to? Return of the Zoomies, with candy, cost 4 x 3 + 4 x 2.50 = $22. The movie Space Flight 3000 cost 4 x 4 + 4 x 1.50 = $22. In order to see either movie, one child is going to give up a box of candy or they have to share 3 boxes of candy. Regardless, this isn't going to help them make a decision so they should just keep arguing.

Is it crazy that a math workbook has a problem with no good solution? There's more math in this problem and more leaning than a whole workbook full of problems like "7 x 3 = ?".

Bonus Question: Since the problem only contains movie and candy, "more than anything" means more than candy. He can offer to be the one who doesn't get a box of candy if they see Return of the Zoomies. There's no guarantee that it will work.

Question 34

He needs to lick it 5,193,875 more times. Your child may already know how to solve this problem, but keep reading.

One of my readers recently asked what is the best way to teach multiplication to a Kindergartener. Do you drill math facts? There are 4 answers. The first answer is that you never ever drill math facts. With each problem, like 4 + 5 or 4 × 5 you let the kid figure it out each and every time until they come up with a mechanism that works for them, and then they are prepared to teach themselves math.

The second answer is that you may have to explain what 4 × 5 is because they've never seen the notation before. I like to introduce something super advanced just for fun and then come back to it a month later.

The third answer is that you ask them draw a picture if a picture will help them put together their thoughts.

The forth answer, the one that applies to this problem, is that you start with something small, like 79 - 4 = ? Then move on to 875 − 4 = ?, 3,875 − 4 = ?, and just keep going until they see the lightbulb. If no lightbulb comes, you just have to try again a month later. It's like when they learned how to read all over again. You never know when C-A-T = "CAT" will stick. This is the single most powerful problem solving and teaching technique in math, and the one I don't see in any of the really great math workbooks that cover problem solving in 5th and 6th grade.

Bonus Question: You've heard the expression, "give a man a fishing pole and not a fish". I'm giving your child a fishing trawler with mile long nets with this question.

First, out loud, subtract 10. Then 20, then 30. This is just a warm up exercise to practice saying the big number. Then subtract 100, 200, 300 all the way to 800. Your child can write down the resulting number. At this point, you can try removing the final 10 tens. This probably won't work. Try subtracting 1000. You subtracted too much. How many more 10's do you need to add back? Help as much as you want, but the child has to say the operations out loud.

However far your child gets with this approach doesn't matter. Just going through it is going to demonstrate to you how we solve big problems in my house and introduce your child to this really powerful technique when they are over their head with math.

Question 35

Yani's grandmother is visiting for 7 x 3 = 21 days, and after 5 days, she will be staying for 21 − 5 = 16 more days.

Bonus Question: The problem doesn't say what Yani is sleeping on. My child said a sleeping bag, but given how goofy this problem is, I say he's sleeping on some curtains.

Question 36

This question is based on a friend whose grandmother visits from Yugoslavia and another friend who opened a cupcake bakery in the site where there was a Romanian chimney cake bakery. It's a situation comedy in the making.

This is also a super duper hard problem, in need of at least one picture after an internet search for an image of a chimney cake and a little background on Romania. This might be a two or three day problem. The most promising solution technique is to break it down into multiple problems and solve each one on the way to the final solution.

The easy way to do this is to start with the 3 + 4 − 5 = 2 chimney cakes that are not eaten. With these 2 chimney cakes, there are 2 x 6 = 12 layers. We need 24 layers, or 24 − 12 = 12 more layers. At this point, a little thinking instead of calculating and the answer is obvious. Yani's grandmother needs to make 2 more chimney cakes.

This is fairly simple math in a ridiculously hard problem. Your child needs to spend 30 minutes just drawing and working the question before getting to the sentence at the end with the question mark. As far as I can tell, this is the key to most of the GAT tests – work the question before starting to work on the answer.

Question 37

The first line has 19 - 9 = 10 people in it. The second line has 6 + 5 = 11 people in it. They should choose the 1st line.

Bonus Question: The version of the problem with circles is called an abstraction. It is used to quickly solve complicated math problems. This is a good time to introduce the term.   The picture must have a building to be correct.

Question 38

There are 12 - 3 = 9 people in front and 8 + 8 = 16 people standing in back. There are 16 - 9 = 7 more people behind them than in front of them.

There is limited repetition in this workbook. Ideally, the child would do the prior problem one day and this problem the next.

Bonus Question: They have to go to the end of the line, which your child may not know until you tell him. After that, there are now 16 + 9 = 25 people standing in front of them. The correct answer to the question is "zero more" or "there are not more people behind them".

Question 39

There are 15 + 18 - 3 = 30 working microwaves, which means Eleanor made 30 cups of tea. It is assumed that she makes a cup of hot tea in each microwave. You may have to boil a cup of water in the microwave to demonstrate what Eleanor is doing because this problem requires your child to think through this whole process. Therefore there are 30 cups of tea – 9 not drunken = 21 workers at the company.   I spent many months sitting with each of my children doing work like this with them, side-by-side until we got to the point where I could just sit there like an average parent sending pointless texts to people in response to their pointless texts, but average parents produce average children so instead sitting here working the problem with my child with the same effort a parent gives during a Read Aloud.

Bonus Question: Now you know.

Super Bonus Question: The kids used 18 + 11 = 29 buckets from 30. 1 bucket is not touched. If the kids put back the popcorn they didn't spill, the answer would be 1 + 3 + 5 = 9. If they cleaned up all of the spilled popcorn and put everything back, the answer is 30. But kids never clean up or put anything back so the answer is 1. My wife informed me that "there are kids who clean things up" and a family discussion ensued. Your answer may vary.

Question 40

I'm tempted to add a test on eye brows at the end of this book. I think a lot of kids are totally not going to get this at first.

This question will take at least an hour just to figure out, and maybe a few days for the social nuances to sink in. Big Eye Brows are defined in the super bonus question. When your child asks what Big Eye Brows mean, tell him to do the bonus question first.

Bill got at least 35 right. The question is what does only a single big eye brown mean? Is it half credit? Good question. Regardless, Bill got Big Eyebrows on at most 100 − 35 −10 = 55 questions, so he missed more than half.

Bonus Question: Self-awareness and self-control are important intrapersonal skills and winning an argument just by making a face even though you are wrong is a social skill. The eyebrow super power will help some children in this area. Other children will just become evil super villains. I forgot I wrote this problem and now my child is staring at me with Big Eyebrows and a smile on his face. He just said "I'm not doing any more math" and is staring at me.

Question 41

There are 2 + 12 = 14 kids on the team. If Mallory goes, this makes 15 kids. If each SUV seats 5, and kids can drive, that would mean 15 / 5 = 3 SUVs. But kids can't drive. Many children are not going to think about this, and this gives you a coaching opportunity. This question is designed to get kids to think about what they read.

The answer for the fewest number of people is 4 + 1 + 4 + 1 + 4 +1 + 3 + 1 = 19, which is what the picture I had to draw to solve this problem. My child drew a picture with 3 full SUVs and then I made him tell me a story of the first SUV, with made up names and the ages of the kids. After it was packed with Lily, Mallory, Ike, Joe, and Ann, I asked him to continue describing in detail how these kids were going to get to the game. Did they put their seat belts on? In which seat was each kid sitting? Who brought the car keys?

Of course, my tester got this problem wrong, which is fine, because I designed it that way. Your child isn't going to break the 90th percentile by getting problems right. No one learns anything with correct answers.

Question 42

First of all, you have to watch the video. Search for "10 year old cup stacking champion". If you have cups, stack them. 3 + 3 + 6 = 12 cups are required. Yani has only 8 + 3 = 11 cups, so the answer is "no".

Many math researchers complain that math workbooks are "mathland", meaning stupid unrealistic boring problems that turn children off to math. I prefer "math fiction", meaning stupid unrealistic problems that are more goofy than boring. You might notice that this works really well for children's literature, so why not in math? If I were teaching a classroom of students, I wouldn't use problems like this. But the purpose of this book is to teach thinking skills and not math. Math is learned accidentally doing this work book, and I was stunned how well math was learned, even though we consistently got incorrect answers.

Question 43

Yani found 20 + 25 = 45 bags. Mallory found 20 + 50 = 70 bags. Since 50 bags are required for the badge, Mallory earned it and Yani didn't.

Bonus Question: Mallory gave Yani 5 bags. She turned in 70 - 5 = 65 and still earned her badge. You may notice in this workbook that Mallory is actually Yani's nemesis, but she is a nice nemesis.

During my child's second attempt to get this problem correct, I noticed tick marks and underlines in the question. We've done about 120 of these problems at this point (many which were rejected for the final versions) and I provided few tips on how to do them, just lots of questions on my part. Six months of problem solving, usually on weekends, and the child is teaching himself solution strategies.

Question 44

Yani has 30 = 15 = 15 licorice pieces. Mallory has 25 – 12 = 13 chocolate bars. Yani has 15 – 13 = 2 more licorice pieces than chocolate bars.

The best way to do this problem is to let your child flounder with the question and solve it in their brain over and over again until they get the correct answer. While this is an awful way to do math, it builds strong cognitive skills. I've found that when many doing problems like this under high stakes, like to earn computer time, children eventually start writing down the equations. We never start with the equations because the floundering causes learning, but writing down equations does not, unless the child comes to this approach on their own.

Bonus Question: Oliver is going to go to grocery stores and ask the store manager for bags.

Question 45

The pizza cost 13 + 3 = 16 dollars. Oliver and Kai have 7 + 7 = 14 dollars. They need 16 - 14 = 2 dollars from Hannah. I thought this was easy but the incorrect answer I got from you-know-who was 16 – 7 = 9.

Bonus Question: Only if they live in Canada. Your child may not realize that most countries (except for Europe) has its own currency. Now might be a good time to close this gap. The reason I include bonus questions like this in here is that there is some kid out there who is capable of getting the first part of the problem correct on two tries within 10 minutes. That won't do for a super hard math workbook.

Question 46

The white chickens laid 9 x 2 = 18 eggs. The brown chickens laid 18 /3 = 6 eggs. This makes 18 + 6 + 5 = 29. There are 15 people in Yani's family, so to have two each requires 15 x 2 = 30.   The answer is no.

Of course, your child will ask "How many people are in Yani's family?", and you will respond "I don't know, I think it was in one of the earlier questions" and hand your child the book.

This is a lot of multiplication and division for a little kid who may not have seen any yet. I recommend a picture or pennies and plenty of time. We keep a jar of pennies around for this purpose.

Question 47

There are 9 – 3 = 6 white chickens in the coop. There are 7 brown chickens in the coop. This makes 6 + 7 = 13 white and brown chickens. If there are 14 chickens in the coop, and there is only one that is not brown or white, then this must be the 14th chicken. Therefore Butterscotch is in the coop.

Bonus Question: There are 3 white chickens in the garden and 10 – 7 = 3 brown chickens in the garden, for a total of 3 + 3 = 6 chickens in the garden. Therefore, there are 14 – 6 = 8 more chickens in the coop than in the garden.

Super Bonus Question: We came up with Bart and Kevin. I hope your child is more creative than that.

Question 48

I recommend that you use pennies or blocks to solve this problem. A careful reading and rereading will turn up the term "exactly" in two places. It's even clunky the second time. Clunkiness is a device that authors use to point out something really important that my child skips right over and ignores.

If a side of the street has an even number, then there is a fence, a yard, or a dividing line "exactly in the middle" of the block. The house has to be on the side of the block with an odd number of houses, and it will be the middle house, or the 8th house.

Bonus Question: Since there are two whole wheat houses on one side of the block that contains the house that ordered the pizza, it is mathematically possible. A rereading of the question provides no other clues. But no one who would live in a house made out of whole wheat bread would eat junk food, and pizza is junk food, so I'm going to say no. But I could be wrong.

Question 49

This is almost a Level 3 question. Plan on mass confusion, lots of time understanding the question and multiple attempts to get the correct answer.

After your child figures out what is going on, his collection is missing 10 - 6 = 4 Zoomie action figures from season 1 and 12 - 9 = 3 Zoomie action figures from season 2. He is missing 4 + 3 = 7. He gets 6 - 3 = 3 new ones, hopefully 3 different ones. Now he is only missing 7 - 3 = 4 Zoomie action figures from season 1 and season 2.

Bonus Question: I have no idea what a Zoomie is. My 10 year old is the source of much of this material. He earns computer time on the weekend by providing question concepts. When your child asks, "What is a Zoomie?", the only answer I have is "Make it up."

Question 50

What hats are the girl penguins wearing? The problem doesn't say. It could be 6 pink hats and 1 green hat. Your child is going to have to decide because the problem does not say. There are 9 green hats (from question #2). If only 1 girl penguin is wearing a green hat and 2 boy penguins are wearing green hats, then there are 9 – 3 = 6 green hats left over. This is an acceptable Level 2 answer.

Bonus Question: Suppose Hannah didn't put all 6 pink hats on the Penguins. There are a few options to solve this problem. There are 7 + 2 = 9 penguins wearing hats. If all 6 pink hats are worn, then there are 9 - 6 = 3 green hats worn, and 9 – 3 = 6 green hats left over. If only 5 pink hats are worn, then 9 – 5 = 4 penguins are wearing green hats, so 9 – 4 = 5 green hats are not worn. If only 4 pink hats are worn, then 9 − 4 = 5 green hats are worn, and 9 − 5 = 4 green hats are not worn. What other options are there?

I'm looking for acknowledgement that there are multiple solutions. Doing them all might be a bit tedious.

The correct answer is 6 (green hats are not worn), 5, 4, 3, 2, 1, or 0. Maybe Hannah put all 9 green hats on the 9 penguins wearing hats. Your child might have started this question with the bonus question approach, since the bonus question is really part of the question.

Math workbooks rarely have problems of this caliber, and the result is the rare child who thinks at this level in math.

Your child might have mentioned that this problem looks a lot like Mr. Popper's Penguins by Richard and Florence Atwater. Reading experts tend to think this is the best book ever written for children. I think the best book is Danny, the Champion of the World by Roald Dahl, because right at the climax there is a big math problem to be solved that is very similar to the ones in Test Prep Math. If you haven't already done so, get The Read-Aloud Handbook: Seventh Edition by Jim Trelease and use it as your At Home Schooling reading guide. Read all of the books and pick your own favorite.

Question 51

I'm going to assume that the circles on the map represent the stones. After the first attempt at drawing the map, you can ask what the circles are. The clues are in the question.

The path with the square stones has 10 + 7 = 17 stones. The path with the round stones has 8 + 8 = 16 stones. He should take the path with the round stones.

Question 52

There are 20 - 3 = 17 arrows that Kai shot that did not hit the target. There are 18 - 4 = 4 arrows that Jeffrey shot that did not hit the target. Kai missed 17 - 4 = 13 more times than Jeffrey.

Question 53

Oliver watched 9 DVDs and read 5 books. He watched 9 - 5 = 4 more DVDs than read books. This question really stumped us because there's nothing tricky going on.

Bonus Question: If I would have come across this question when I was a child, I wouldn't have spent every night hiding under a blanket. The answer is that there are no monsters that want to live in Oliver's lame closet. They have much more interesting places to live like the sewer or dark castles or the school cafeteria. Both of my kids are afraid of the dark especially after reading the creepy books I bring home from the library. They are scared of the dark because of their big imaginations, and this book doesn't help.

Question 54

Wow! What a hard problem! I am not aware of any part of math curriculum that uses this concept until differential calculus, although changing speed would qualify. If your child is really struggling, cross out or cover up "between his best and worst times" and then you'll see how much did "the difference change". The difference on Monday is 15 - 8 = 7. The difference on Tuesday is 12 - 7 = 5. Therefore, the difference decreased by 2 between Monday and Tuesday.

Question 55

The piano should have 61 – 25 = 36 white keys, but it only has 36 – 7 = 29 white keys. Therefore it has 29 – 25 = 4 more white keys than black keys.

Bonus Question: I tried to explain to my son when he entered the fourth grade why the Clarinet was the most awesome of all instruments, and I showed him my 2 clarinets, one for me, and one for him. He chose the trumpet.   I explained to my younger son that he will play the clarinet and there will be no discussion.

As a prerequisite for the problem coming up after the next problem, make sure the picture of the keyboard is 36 white keys wide so that the black keys fit within the width of the white keys.

Question 56

If the key was really 5 inches long, then the answer should be a board that is 1 inch wide, 7 x 5 = 35 inches long, and the same depth as the key.

Bonus Question: In this case, Hannah needs a board that is 4 x 15 = 60 inches long. So he ended up buying 120 – 35 = 85 more wood.

Super Bonus Question: If you look at a saw, you'll see that the teeth have the dimension of width, and these teeth are going to remove this width completely from a board. I learned this the hard way when I replaced my window trim myself.   It was an eye opener that a saw has width.

Question 57

If the month is June, then the month has 30 days and each half has 30 ÷ 2 = 15 days.   In the first half of the month, Hannah took off 15 − 12 = 3 days. In the second half of the month, Hannah took off 15 − 9 = 6 days. Hannah took off 6 − 3 = 3 more days in the second half of the month.

Bonus Question: How is "regularly" defined for piano practice for a 7 to 9 year old?   Does it matter that she started with 6 days a week and then went down to 4 or 5? Personally, at this age, I'm happy with 4 days of anything because I'm already dealing with the long term consequences of over doing it, but I know little girls whose parents have to put limits on practicing. Feel free to steer the discussion however you see fit.

Question 58

The 1st time, Kai hit 16 - 11 = 5 cups. The 119th time, he hit 16 - 4 = 12 cups. He hit 12 - 5 = 7 more cups the 119th time than the first time.

Bonus Question: Yani is not happy because his cup stacking cups now have holes in them. Kai's parents are not happy because he stayed up to 4pm + 7 hours = 11pm on a school night. Hopefully, you are now comfortable with incorrect answers. Your child's success depends on it.

Question 59

Yani has 11 - 3 = 8 pig pieces and 13 - 5 = 8 chicken pieces. He found 8 + 8 = 16 origami animal pieces.

Notice the difference between this question and a standard math facts worksheet.   If the child has to do this question multiple times because it is slightly convoluted and overly complex, the result is 10 math facts or more. I found from doing this workbook that math facts took care of themselves.

Question 60

After you have a discussion with your child that complaining does not count as practicing, Yani practiced for 35 - 23 = 12 minutes on Monday, and 29 - 15 = 14 minutes on Tuesday. He practiced for 14 -12 = 2 more minutes on Tuesday.

Bonus Question: He can quit complaining. If your child is not complaining about how hard this book is, rest assured that Section 2 made my brain hurt.

Question 61

There are 12 parts named in the question. Each one requires 3 bolts, for a total of 3 x 12 = 36 bolts. For fun, your child can create a "times 3" calculator just by writing down the multiples of 3 on a pieces of paper. This helps some kids organize the concept of multiplication. Mallory and the real Lily found 7 + 3 = 10 bolts. There are 36 - 10 = 26 bolts missing.

Bonus Question: This won't work with a picture so you actually have to get a real nut and a matching bolt. There are two obvious numbers - the number of threads on the bolt, and the number of treads inside the nut. Spend plenty of time discussing the definition of "thread". The nut and bolt might have a hexagon or other shape. The math questions to add or subtract the numbers.

My question was "How many more threads are on the bolt than the nut".

The best question is "How many nuts can you fit on the bolt."

The super bonus question which you can give is "How many times do you have to turn the nut to get it on the all the way?"

Here's the back story for the bonus question. I just read the latest Jo Boaler book. She's the leader of the math revolution and a member of the Competitive Parent Hall of Fame. My material differs from the material she recommends to teach math concepts, because this book has a different objective. In her book, she mentioned that mathematicians spend most of their time asking questions, but students spend most of their time answering questions. She referenced the "nut and bolt" question. You could teach multiplication and division using nuts and bolts if you're interested. You can find the nut and bold curriculum on the internet.

Question 62

There are 19 - 6 = 13 band members who don't play brass instruments. There are 13 - 6 = 7 people in the audience who don't like brass. There are 13 + 7 = 20 people who don't like brass or who play an instrument that is not brass.

My recommendation for this question is to start with an internet video of a big band. Spend some time covering terms like jazz, percussion, woodwind, brass, and ask your child if any instruments are missing (strings). The missing strings are the difference between the term orchestra and the term "big band".

If it is not going well, a picture is needed, complete with instruments. I would use a picture if my child's skill set is incomplete, which it will likely be if he is only on problem 14 of this book. If you dig through my blog, you'll see a picture of the Origami Jazz band that my kids created while watching a big band at the Jazz Showcase. You'll also see a picture of an amazing jazz singer with my editor and my question research department.

This question is packed with skills. The most important of these skills are not technical:

1. Interest in something unusual.

2. Oblivious to how long the problem will take.

3. Logic, represented by all of the "nots"

4. Solving 3 equations in one problem (working memory) in the face of convoluted logic.

5. Doing a problem that is way harder than either the test or school.

6. Having to develop "figuring out" skills because no one is helping.

Question 63

There are 4 reusable paper cups in a commemorative cup. $4 \times 25 = 100$ cents, which equals a dollar. Yani earned $20/5 = 4 + 7 = 11$ dollars. Mallory earned $(8 / 4 = 2) + (7 \times 2 = 14) = 2 + 14 = 16$. Yani has to sell $16 + 1 - 11 = 6$ more commemorative cups.

Bonus Question: The question doesn't provide any help, so the correct answer is "I don't know." You can tell your child that later in the book, you'll find out why Yani did not sell the additional 6 cups.

"Dealing with Ambiguity" is a big part of GAT tests, but on a GAT test, the child has to resolve the ambiguity. We do some of that here, but to outdo the GAT test, I invented "Unresolvable Ambiguity".

Question 64

There are $13 - 3 = 10$ registration forms for girls. Mallory found 8. It is possible that all of these registration forms are from girls, in which case the largest possible number of registration forms for boys that are missing is 8.

To help your child approach this question, you can ask "Guess how many registration forms Mallory found for girls and boys?" "I don't know, the question doesn't say" is a good response, but the child still has to guess 2 numbers and solve the question. Then repeat this process to cover all possible choices, including 8 registration forms for girls and 0 for boys, which yields the answer.

Bonus Question: $8 - 4 = 4$ boys are missing registration forms. There are $8 - 4 = 4$ registration forms found for girls, which means $13 - 2 - 4 = 7$ girls are missing registration forms, since 2 of them never turned in registration forms. It's arguable whether these 2 girls are missing forms or have blank forms in their possession.

Question 65

First, there are 14 bananas. After tapping there are 14 - 9 = 5 bananas, but then she bought 5 more so there are 5 + 5 = 10. Then there are 6 - 3 = 3 more for a total of 10 + 3 = 13.

At this point, a reasonable pace for this problem would be 20 minutes to understand it, 5 minutes of discussion, 5 more minutes of reading the problem, and 10 minutes of figuring out the solution, and 3 attempts at the solution.

Bonus Question: In the first section of the question, Hannah gets 9 - 5 = 4 gold coins, and in the next section she gets 3 more gold coins, for a total of 4 + 3 = 7 gold coins. She has 13 - 7 = 6 fewer gold coins than bananas.

Super Bonus Question: First, ask your child to explain the rules to you and then guess what Oliver will say. Oliver's actual answer was that this is the lamest video game ever.

I rejected most of the questions my Question Research Department came up with that involved video games. There were dozens of these. This one was so ridiculous that I decided to include it.

Question 66

In the first few weeks, the brothers and sisters got 120 = 70 = 50. In February, Yani got 70 + 60 = 130, and his brothers and sisters got 50 + 80 = 130. Yani got 130 - 130 = 0 more Dojo points than the rest of his family combined.

Bonus Question: They bought one for Yani. If one other kid had 100 Dojo points or more, that would make 2 Slurpees. It is also possible than no kid got more than 10. So either 1 or 2.

There are 2 competing skills that will get a child a 99% on standardized tests in early grades. One is going slowly and carefully, given time constraints. The other skill is accommodating deficits in "going slowly and carefully" by doing every problem 2 or 3 times to make sure it is correct. The SAT requires a balance of these skills plus a third - identifying questions that require revisiting before time is up. The intent of this book is to build "going slowly and carefully" and the "redo" skills at the same time.

Super Bonus Question: The answer is 130 - 100 = 30. You have 3 choices with this question. You can spend 30 more minutes modeling "biggest possible", you can just state that the other unnamed kid got 100 Dojo points, or you can just help do the problem. I put this question in to penalize any child who releases working memory when he thinks he is finished with the question.

If working memory could be developed by running sprints at the end of practice, then I'm one of those mean coaches who makes the kid do yet another sprint because he wasn't happy with the effort on the last one.

Question 67

This is not an easy question to understand for some kids. You may need to step through it a few times until the child understands we need a list of activities to fill 60 - 7 = 53 minutes. Lily's list has 12 + 12 + 20 = 44 minutes. She needs 53 - 44 = 9 minutes of boredom filling activities.

Question 68

Mallory beat him 7 + 4 = 11 times at school, and 6 + 9 = 15 times outside of school. She beat him 15 - 11 = 4 fewer times at school than outside of school.

Bonus Question. This is a hard problem to address logically. Since he hasn't actually won the competition, his essay doesn't follow the rules because things haven't turned out "good" when he submitted his essay. But if he does win, then things will turn out good. Whatever your child says is fine.

It turns out that Yani was the only one who submitted an essay with a qualifying challenge. The worst thing that happened in the other essays was that one kid was 15 minutes late to school because his mom didn't have the right brand of turkey for his sandwich and had to run to the grocery store. Another kid only got to use the computer for 15 minutes on the weekend. So Yani won.

Question 69

If he got 22 - 8 = 14, 14 + 11 = 25, he doesn't not have enough. Your child may argue that Oliver bought ornaments that didn't light up despite what was implied in the question.   Indulge the argument because it is a good thing.

Bonus Question: Olivier doesn't give one to himself, so he gave out 28 − 1 = 27. He was 3 short from the prior problem, so 3 kids got ornaments that didn't light up.

Question 70

He has 20 - 9 + 4 - 3 = 12. He needs 25 - 12 = 13 more gold coins before he will sell his collection.

Warning: Do not help with the bonus question.

Bonus Question: There is a high probability your child cannot answer this question.   Leave the child alone for a while. Hopefully, they will read the Super Bonus Question on their own out of desperation or boredom. If not, you can make suggest that they try to answer that one.

Super Bonus Question: The numbers in this question and the Tap the Banana question are identical.

It appears that the Tap the Banana game is magical and the gold coins used in the game come from Sumi Von Gusa's coin collection.

Question 71

There are 18 / 2 = 9 girls next to Lily Robot, and 28 - 18 = 10 boys in class, so 10 / 2 = 5 boys are next to Lily Robot. 9 - 5 = 4 more girls are next to Lily Robot than boys.

Bonus Question: This question is designed to turn your child into a mathematician. Hopefully, your child forgot all of the numbers and has no clue what to do. The 2 things that mathematicians do that normal people don't do is a) think a lot and b) solve hard problems with a really easy version of the problem first.

You child can use a blank piece of paper to answer this question. The book is closed.

You can remind your child how the teacher splits up kids in class as many times as needed. Suppose there are 2 boys and 2 girls in class, how many more kids are standing on the 2 walls next to Lily Robot (who is in the corner) than the two walls across from Lily Robot? Suppose there are 4 girls and 2 boys, or 6 boys and 2 girls, or 4 boys and 4 girls.   Just keep doing this exercise until the light bulb goes off, and then you have a mathematician.

Question 72

You might need to refer to the super bonus question from the Sumi Von Gusa's gold coin problem when your child is completely stumped.   When vegetables appear on Kai's screen, they disappear from Yani's mother's garden. There are 8 - 5 = 3 carrots that have disappeared, and 12 - 7 = 5 heads of lettuce that have disappeared from the garden.   That means that 3 + 5 vegetables appear on the screen.

Super Bonus Question: Kai's mom takes away the video game and hides it.

This story almost has a moral, but not quite.

Question 73

I had to visit www.nebraskacorn.org to find out what it shucked off of an ear of corn, and I'm still not sure that "ear leaf" is the correct term. The left leg has 7 x 4 = 28 of these things, and the right leg has 4 x 4 = 16. There are 28 - 16 = 12 more ear leaves on his left pant leg than his right.

My Question R&D department challenged me to use "corn peel pants" in a question. I'm Ok with that because the Test Prep Writers Code forbids a test prep workbook without a question specifically for Iowa. Iowans probably die their corn peel pants black and gold or cardinal and gold.

Bonus Question: The right sock is pulled way up because the right pant leg is shorter and it is tucked into the right sock. There is no way a child is going to be able to answer this bonus question without a picture of Sumi Von Gusa wearing corn peel pants.

Question 74

There were 4 + 9 + 8 + 2 + 4 = 27 tubes of food.

The goal of this bonus question is a skill more advanced than direct calculation and working memory. Once your child starts calculating, ask them to stop. Cover the middle paragraph beginning with "When they..." and then ask the child to answer the question.

Bonus Question: The correct answer, with no calculation, is Mallory, because she always beats Yani at everything. To verify the answer, Yani grabbed 4 + 9 = 13 tubes of food, and Mallory grabbed 8 + 2 + 4 = 14 tubes of food.

Question 75

There are 17 - 9 = 8 people who are not cup stacking champions. There are 23 - 11 = 12 other pictures that are not pictures of cups. Assuming that these 8 + 12 = 20 pictures do not have to do with cup stacking, the answer is 20.

Bonus Question: Cups are stacked on tables, and therefore have to do with cup stacking competitions. That means 3 less pictures have nothing to do with cup stacking competitions, so the new answer is 20 - 3 = 17. Or your child can just resolve the whole problem. My recommendation for this question, after your child is totally baffled and gets it wrong, is to say "draw a picture of a person stacking cups. Are they stacking cups in the air? On a turtle?"

Question 76

There are (6 + 7 = 13) x 2 = 26 eyes in the first book and (7 + 5 + 3 = 15) x 2 = 30 eyes in the second book. The first book has 30 - 26 = 4 fewer eyes.

Bonus Question: Hopefully, this question required a bit of thinking and no calculating. I always get calculating, and always ask the child to do it again slowly without recalculating. The second book has 4 more ears because there are the same number of eyes as ears in the book.

Note that if your child did this problem correctly, the child did 6 arithmetic problems. If your kids are like mine, by the time they get the right answer, they did 24 or 30 calculations because they need multiple attempts to get the problem wrong. If you like worksheets, this single problem is a worksheet.

Question 77

The pot holds 8 cups and is full. When the 6 cups are poured, 2 x 6 more cups magically appear in the pot, but it only has room for 6 more, so 12 - 6 = 6 cups are on the table. There are also 6 cups in the tea cups on the table, for a total of 6 + 6 = 12 cups on the table, the floor, or in a cup.

Bonus Question: The pot has 8 cups, so the answer is 12 - 8 = 4.

Super Bonus Question: When you work through this exercises with various guesses you'll see that it is 2. Guessing one of the 5 core problem solving approaches.

This question delves in "pure math", aka number theory. My kids hate "pure math". I tried advanced math books of this type for young kids until I discovered Rule #1 Of Parenting: Anything you encourage and provide extra material for the kids will come to hate, because it is uncool and old fashioned, for you the parent are by definition uncool and old fashioned. Therefore, I give them problems like these that are not math and stay as far away from their school math as possible. They've already determined that this is not math, and that's OK with me.

Question 78

Yani has 15 - 8 = 7 extra tickets. He would like to invite 3 + 3 - 6 other people. He has enough extra tickets. If your child assumes that the parents are going, extra points for thinking, and the answer may vary.

Bonus Question: This is a quick working memory sprint especially when your child sees the word "cats". Yani only has 1 extra ticket left so the answer is no. Elicit the response "cats can't go anyway" or ask "what if they could go?" depending on which route your child goes so that no matter what answer they give it's wrong.

Question 79

9 - 3 = 6 yellow kites are still in the air.   8 of the blue kites are flying. 8 - 6 = 2 more blue kites are in the air.

Bonus Question: Where do kites come from? Probably a major retailer or drug store chain.   Imaging going to one of these places to get a kite for your child. Are you going to find 9 yellow kites, or even 9 kites with printed designs or colors that are primarily yellow, or even 9 kites that are remotely the same primary color? That's totally silly.

What is not silly is doing all of this thinking and explaining this to your child.   They will of course not know what you are talking about nor could they have thought of this themselves, but they will learn a valuable lesson that there is probably another answer there lurking deep in the question.

Question 80

If the watch beeps 15 times a day, then it has 15 - 6 - 8 = 1 beep left. It did not beep before the spelling be. Oliver should be worried.

However, it could have beeped on Oliver's turn.   If Oliver spelled his word correctly, he is worried. If Oliver spelled his word incorrectly, he is not worried. If a second grade child can get to 15 - 8 - 6 = 1, then that's pretty good. Dissect the problem one sentence at a time asking questions along the way. "What happened on Oliver's turn? How do you know that? Where does it say that in the question?"

The best approach to math and the only approach to a cognitive skills test is this: "I'm going to be tricked by the question and then get it wrong." That attitude is the path to confidence and ultimate success. Occasionally a parent of a young child will ask, "Why did my child score 99% on the standardized test but only 50% on the cognitive skills test?" This question is replaced a few years later by "Why did my child fall on the standardized math test from 99% to 75%?" In both cases, the gap is thinking skills and the shortest path to thinking skills is "I'm going to be tricked by the question and then get it wrong."

Question 81

There are lots of clever ways to solve this problem and they all involve grouping.   When I get the answer to this problem from my child, asking about his grouping strategy, my response is "Good, show me a different way to do the problem." I always get my money's worth out of math workbooks.

The way I did this problem is to translate quarters and dollars into Dinky Binky Trolls. There are $14 \div 2 = 7$ trolls from quarters and $4 \div 2 = 2$ trolls from dollars. We're going to lose $\$1.25 \div \$0.50 = 2\frac{1}{2}$ trolls from the soda, and we're left with $7 + 2 - 2\frac{1}{2} = 6\frac{1}{2}$ trolls. Since we can't buy ½ of a troll, Lily will end up with 6 trolls.

Bonus Question: This is my favorite question in the book. If your child is an experienced mathematician, the best answer would be draw a Dinky Binky Troll, which is derived from a similar question earlier in the book and involves no hard work or calculating. This is the genius that we are hoping for. Non mathematicians call this "laziness" but mathematicians call this "genius".

Question 82

Yani needs 25, and after he picks the bilberries, he will have 5 + 9 + 14 = 28. So he doesn't need any more.

Bonus Question. After a quick internet search, cowberries and bilberries are native to Northern Europe and don't appear exist in North America. They could be in North America under different names, in which case the terms would be different in this question.

Strawberries originated in Chile (not 100% sure) but were transported and grown everywhere. It looks like this forest is in Northern Europe, or it just happens to have a wide variety of berries.

My kids had a lot of questions for the bonus question, which is good. Are these berries made up? Is this another planet? What about the hooded figure? He is not helpful, and the berries are the only other important element to the question. The question I put to them was "How would you go about solving this problem?" not "What is the answer?" The answer I'm looking for is "Look up bilberry on the internet and find out where it is." but I never got that, even from a 5th grader. So I showed them, and hopefully when a question like this appears, the first thing they should do is look it up on the internet.

Super Bonus Question: I have no clue. It might be because the forest is close to the temple of Zoomirantuk.

Question 83

So far he has 9 - 4 = 5 non Honey Bite candies, plus 19 - 9 = 10, and 10 - 3 = 7 more, so he has 15 + 7 = 12 candies that aren't Honey Bites. He needs 25 - 12 = 13 more.

Here's how I would figure out the rest of the problem, which is impossible by the way, if I was 7 years old. If he went to one more house, it could be a Honey Bite or not. If he went to 2 more houses, he's getting one Honey Bite and one candy that is not Honey Bite. Then try 3. By the time the child gets to 26 more, she has either figured out how this works or got the right answer. Starting with an easy version of the problem is our go-to solution method for hard problems. The secret to getting kids to adopt this approach is to convince them that problems take both a) a long time and b) many attempts.

Bonus Question: Honey Bites are my pseudonym for the worst candy in the world. I used to cringe when I got one of these while trick-or-treating.

Question 84

I'm going to guess that Oliver got 25 Polish Lobster Candies. I'm not 100% sure, but clearly Oliver lives in an unusual neighborhood. Yani has 11 + 8 = 19 Polish Lobster Candies, so Yani probably has 25 - 19 = 6 fewer Polish Lobster Candies.

A classmate of one of my children lives on the West side of Chicago. After Trick-Or-Treating, his mom sent us a picture of his candy haul - among the Polish and Russian candy, none of it in English, was lobster candy. We were all immediately jealous. Next year, we're hitting the West side, including dinner. I think of it as a short, cheap proxy for a European vacation. If you live in Chicago and trick-or-treat on the west side, look for a father of 2 children who is yelling "I asked for the probability distribution, not the space of preferences!"

Question 85

If they used all of the slices, then Hannah used 18 - 11 = 7 slices of turkey and Kai used 17 - 10 = 7 slices of roast beef. Kai has 11 + 7 = 18 slices and Hannah has 10 + 7 = 17. Kai has 18 - 17 = 1 more slice.

Question 86

The Polyphonic Shree is a thinly veiled math parody of the Polyphonic Spree, which I occasional see in concert because they are insane and my wife owns many of their CD's. Plus they have enough members for a good math problem. This year, they want 9 + 8 x 2 = 27. Last year they had 15 + 10 = 25. They want 27 - 25 = 2 more. I hope your child is attempting to do these problems without writing anything. Bad math practice, but good thinking practice. Also, I hope you're searching for images of every new concept, like Lobster Candy. Diversions make math more like math.

Question 87

We actually tried this and it takes a lot of size D batteries for a small amount of Christmas tree lights. We were going to do this for Halloween, but the size D batteries needed were way too heavy to carry around. Next year, I'm going to do this on a wagon or something.

I got this idea from going to a Polyphonic Spree concert and carefully observing a guy wrapped in a white sheet and Christmas tree lights. He was hard to miss because he was head bobbing more than anyone else and it was distracting. The head bobbing, not the lights. His 4 batteries were way bigger than size D and if I thought a bit, I wouldn't have wasted money on the size D battery I bought.

By drawing a picture, you can figure out that there are 30 / 5 = 6 lights per battery. Hopefully you did the bolt question which warms your child up for multiplication. 42 - 30 = 12 more lights will require 12 /6 = 2 more batteries, or just draw a picture

Question 88

There are 12 red cups to begin with. Then she added 4 red cups so now she has 12 + 4 = 16. The blue cups are 3 x 2 = 6. The difference is 16 - 6 = 10. Half of that is 5. So she has 16 - 5 = 11.

Give your child a whole hour to complete this question. Don't even ask for an answer until they've done the problem 3 times (both reading and doing) and are absolutely, absolutely sure

Bonus Question: Ask for clues. She is his nemesis and a hero can't go on in the story without his Nemesis. Therefore Mallory will go anyway, or not. But it's irrelevant because she never loses to Yani so he will guess incorrectly.

Question 89

This problem should take a long time to solve. On the first reading, "at least" might be ignored. A bright child might ask "what does at least mean?" in the context of this question and a bright parent would respond "You tell me".

Mallory will at least be at space 5 + 2 = 7, and Lily will at least be at space 3 + 2 + 2 = 7. So Mallory and Lily will be on the same space if they get the lowest Zombie card. Is Mallory ahead of Lily? Maybe. Either child could get a bonus card with a 3 and the other 2's, so it could go either way. If the bonus cards could be 2, 3, 4, 5, or 6, what are the possible outcomes? To "learn" the math of this question properly, a child has to make a chart of possible outcomes until they get it. To learn the thinking skill for this question, the child has to discover and come to terms with the concept "at least".

This can be frustrating problem because it introduces uncertainty. Once your child picks up on uncertainty, regular problems in math books become boring. Fortunately, math curriculum is quickly changing so hopefully in a few years, most math problems in math books will not be focused on a single problem with a single boring solution. If your child's math curriculum has not caught up yet to the new teaching methods, buy Jo Boaler's Mindsets book and she'll point you in the right direction for better material.

Question 90

First of all, it is 100% true that you don't learn something when you get a problem correct and you can announce this to your child with 100% confidence. This workbook is slightly different in that you learn a lot by not getting the correct understanding of the question on the first reading and have to read it again before you try to solve the problem. Then you get it wrong. I learned that from cognitive skills tests.

Yani got 30 - 11 = 19 correct, and Mallory got 30 - 4 - 4 = 22 correct. Mallory got 22 - 19 = 3 more answers correct. Conversely, Mallory got 11 - 4 - 4 = 3 more answers correct, but I doubt that kids will use this approach.

Bonus Question. Yes. Yani learned 11 - 4 - 4 = 3 more things than Mallory. Yani finally beat Mallory at something.

Question 91

Yani practiced the song 23 + 17 = 40 times. Oliver practiced the song 10 + 10 = 20 times. Yani is twice as good as Oliver because he practiced twice as much. If your child guesses, make them prove it mathematically, and reiterate the point about practicing.

Bonus Question: I'll let you two think about this question for a few minutes. The question to think about is "what are the possible things that could have happened?" Feel free to accept any answer after a discussion and move on to the next question.

Question 92

He practiced 200 + 400 = 600 times when wet and 1000 - 200 - 400 - 300 = 100 times in his bedroom and 300 + 100 = 400 times while dry. Or 1000 - 600 = 400 times dry if your child is really thinking.

Bonus Question: A careful rereading of the question shows that this kid practiced the song 300 times on the bus. The other kids used to yell at him to stop. The girl that sits next to him went insane. One kid threw his shoe. The driver quit. Three parents pulled their children out of the school. All of the kids' grades fell because they couldn't get that annoying song out of their heads during tests.

Question 93

There are 4 + 7 + 8 + 6 = 25 pickles. Yani needs 8 x 2 + 8 x 2 = 32 healthy snacks. Once he grabs all of the pickles, he needs 32 - 25 = 7 carrots.

Bonus Question: He forgot to pack clothes and his tooth paste.

Super Bonus Question: The first problem is that Yani is packing cupcakes and donuts and his mother lets him. The second problem is that there is a jar of pickles in the garden. If your child is really working the question, then these things will have come up already. If your child is just doing the math, then she has to read the problem again more carefully.

"Working the Question" is the most important skill in school, on standardized tests, on GAT tests, and in physics research. It's half of the battle.

Question 94

After Yani's turn, he has 10 + 5 = 15 mints and 10 - 5 = 5 raisins. Oliver has 5 mints and 15 raisins. After Oliver's turn, he has 5 + 3 = 8 mints and 15 - 3 = 12 raisins. Yani has 15 - 3 = 12 mints and 8 raisins. Oliver has 8 mints and Yani has 8 raisins, so the answer is zero.

Bonus Question: If Yani and Oliver both like mints, than the answer is Yani. But Yani or Oliver might like raisins more. In fact, if both players either like raisins or mints more, then it is not clear who won until we leave arithmetic math and go into game theory math. There are 4 options and 4 ways to evaluate who won. Game theory is much more fun, more interesting, and far more useful than arithmetic in the information age, but our school curriculum is stuck in the early 19th century and leads to calculus. Calculus would be great if all the bridges weren't already built, but they are already built.

For older kids, there are even more options. A player might like both equally, or neither. The player who likes neither loses if he is stuck with more of the total.

For graduate students, their raisin/mint preferences need to be modelled with equations.

Returning to this book and its purpose, "Who won" can be answered in lots of ways for a thinking child, or a child who is learning to think, and that makes math a whole lot more fun than "7 + 3 = ?", the poster equation for boredom.

Question 95

You may have to search "parts of a cactus" to find out what a spine is. When your child asks "what's a spine" you are supposed to reply "guess or I don't know, let's look it up." Lily has 5 + 12 - 8 = 9 spines in her hands. Mallory has 7 + 5 - 8 = 4 spines in her hands. Mallory has 9 - 4 = 5 fewer spines in her hands.

Bonus Question: Before they removed the spines, Lily had 17 and Mallory had 12, so Mallory had 17 - 12 = 5 fewer spines. I was tempted to ask a bonus question "why are they playing kickball with a barrel cactus?" but the only answer I could come up with is "because the author is crazy".

Super Bonus Question: It's the same answer because...wait for the ahah moment which never comes with my sons. It's the same answer because they removed the same amount. Feel free to spend a day or 2 coming to terms with the "why".

I found with Level 3 that you can give a child nothing but problems like this - no math facts, no addition/subtraction worksheets - and they'll hit 99% in math. I speculate that the reason why is that school gives facts and worksheets and my child just has a high interest level in math because it's so darn fun. Plus he always gets the wrong answer multiple times which I don't even bother grading sometimes, so there's no sense of discouragement. The irony.

Super Duper Bonus Question: The saguaro, I'm guessing, because it becomes much, much bigger. Unless it's a baby saguaro, in which case the barrel cactus. Time for a science trip to the Grand Canyon to count spines.

Question 96

The guppy tank ends up with 13 - 5 = 8 guppies. A guppy is a small tropical fish. The minnow tank has 12 + 5 - 3 = 14 small fish. There are 14 - 6 = 8 more small fish in the minnow tank than the guppy tank.

I've decided that this question represents the limit of working memory. Any more than this requires a written framework to keep track of things. A written model takes the work out of math and reduces it to arithmetic. School math teaches written frameworks, but this workbook sticks with thinking.

Question 97

There are 21 - 6 - 7 = 8 people by the tank that are not firemen. Since Oliver is there, then 8 - 1 people are clowns. Oliver is the key, or else your child with think that there are 8 clowns. If your child forgets Oliver, you can read this question one phrase at a time with your child.

Bonus Question: "What exactly" needs an internet search of an image of a fish tank. The water is not on fire, unless there's an oil spill. I don't like the "oil spill" concept because it's more of a brain teaser since the problem doesn't mention oil. The water and the things in the water are out. It's unlikely the glass is on fire. That leaves the plastic on the side, the filter motor, or the light. I'm leaning toward motor or light.

Question 98

Since this book is only level 2, I'm willing to take almost any answer as long as the child understands the question. If the child gets answer in 10 minutes or less, however, it's time to raise the bar. If your child gets this problem correct on the first try, all I can say is I'll get my revenge on the bonus questions if you promise not to help.

The question neglects to mention that when you stack buckets, the top row has 1 less bucket than the bottom row because you have to stack a bucket on top of 2 buckets or it will fall over. If your child draws a picture with 7 buckets stacked on top of 7 buckets, you can have a little discussion. Ideally, you have plastic cups from the Cup Stacking Competition questions and you can have your child experiment with full cups of water like a Montessori school, or use empty cups if you don't want a mess. If you don't have plastic cups lying around, hand the child 4 glasses and ask for a demonstration.

The clowns had 7 + 6 = 13 filled buckets, and the firemen had 5 + 4 + 3 = 12 buckets. The clowns won.

Bonus Question: The clowns won because they practice clown acts with buckets full of confetti. The firemen never use buckets because they have hoses. The clowns have more practice, and practice makes them better. This is a brain teaser, although a simple one, because it is easy to figure out if you discuss the question over a matter of days and take each word one at a time.

Question 99

You may need to help with the definition of "place setting". He started with 14 x 2 = 28 + 1 = 29 cups. The he lost 5 x 2 cups and now has 29 - 10 = 18 cups. He lost 18 /3 = 6, so he is left with 18 - 6 = 12. Oliver's uncle is going to become the coach.

This is a nice step-by-step problem, good for concentration and diligence.

Bonus Question: Oliver's uncle already had 12 cups so he was going to coach anyway.

Which child is going to do better in math? A child who is 100% confident in their abilities and work performance, or a child who doubts their own answer, or a child who learns to mistrust and skepticism of my trickery. All 3 of these are built into the problem.

Super Bonus Question: Sumi Von Gusa, of course. Who else would have an elephant in their house?

Question 100

Each foot of the small weights 13 tons / 13 feet = 1 ton. If you slice the small statue vertically into 13 sections of 1 foot each, then each section should weigh 1 ton. Similarly, each foot of the big statue weighs 96 / 32 = 3 tons. Each foot of the big statue weighs 3 − 1 = 2 more tons. The big statue actually weighs only 84 tons, but I rounded up.

Bonus Question: Easter Island.

Super Bonus Question: It depends where you live. In the US, a ton weighs 2000 pounds, but in the United Kingdom, a ton weighs 2,240 pounds. In the rest of Europe, a ton weighs something else. Research on Easter Island was not conclusive, even on scholar websites, because the type of ton used is never mentioned.

Section 2

Question 1

I made this problem ridiculously easy just to make children comfortable with the concept of "F". It still might take a few months before they really get the concept of F. You should have your child do one or 2 problems every week or every 2 weeks until they get it. Then the problems get ridiculously hard so that they take me 5 minutes to solve one problem. The best way to prepare for these problems is to do the word problems, but these "F" problems can be so painful that I decided on working them in occasionally while the child does word problems, and then hopefully they can do a word problem one day and one of these the next day.

If your child is really stuck with this section and becomes frustrated, my first question is did she spend 20 minutes trying to solve a problem? The word problems are resetting expectations that a single problem takes 20 minutes to figure out. Until you and your child get to this point, you can't move on to advanced math or get to the 99th percentile. Once you learn patience with the question, then anything is possible.

A. 9

B. 12

C. 10

D. 9

E. 21

F. 8

Question 2

The purpose of this question is to set up challenges in later questions. These are going to get very complicated later in the book. You can provide some help on the first few problem types. Later in the book, any one of these problems might take a whole session.

You may be tempted to help because your child is stuck. This is OK if your child is stuck after 15 minutes of thinking. Later in the book raise the bar to 25 minutes.

A. 5

B. 11

C. 0

D. 15

E. 6

F. 10

Question 3

Each of these solutions could be either multiplication/division or addition/subtraction. The child won't know which until reviewing the answer set. You can ask questions like "Could it be anything else?". The first time the child sees a problem like this, he will get it wrong and be totally baffled. I don't know how anyone gets questions like these right when they see it for the first time on a cognitive skills test.

A. 6

B. 19

C. 4

D. 10

E. 4

F. 1

Question 4

A. 15

B. 14

C. 3

D. 3

E. 16

F. 27

Question 5

This question slowly ramps up on the number of mental operations to solve for F.

A. 15

B. 11

C. 0

D. 4

E. 1

F. 19

Question 6

These questions throw a curve ball (again). Your child is comfortable with "F = + 4" or "F = - 8" and suddenly the answer is "F = x 3" or "F = / 3". This is exactly the type of confusion that a cognitive skills test would do to a 5 year old, so it's fair game for an 8 or 9 year old. The question isn't "what is the difference between the 2 numbers" but "what is the relationship of the 2 numbers." Or, if you are desperate, just point out that there are 4 arithmetic operators and please feel free to experiment with all of them.

Answer number 1 could be "F = + 4" or "F = x 2", and the child won't know until he gets it wrong. The skills I'm looking for is to get the wrong answer and try again. I'm tempted to make a whole page of multiplication and division, but I'm looking for the skill of identifying something surprising, not whether or not your young child can multiply or divide.

A. 16

B. 17

C. 6

D. 15

E. 6

F. 4; F = " ÷ 4 "

Question 7

A. 8 Did your child noticed anything different about the question?

B. 3

C. 3

D. 20

E. 30

F. 1

Question 8

A. 40; If you child doesn't notice the "F F" or is confused by it, just continue reading the newspaper. Shrug your shoulders. Don't give any hints.

B. 0

C. 12

D. 5

E. 10

F. 24

Question 9

This question is level 2 for this type of problem. I got complaints from readers that these questions are really hard so I'm trying to go slow and add repetition.   The two main skills needed for this question, besides going slow and doing the problem over, are abstraction (dealing with the F) and working memory. Every time multiplication is thrown in, like F = " x 3", three more skills are exercised, provided it's a surprise.

A. 11

B. 9; F is "/3". I had to tell my own children that they should be prepared to try "+/-" and "x/÷" on every problem. This is a common trick on cognitive tests.

C. 14; F = " − 6"

D. 0

E. 19

F. 2

Question 10

A. 9

B. 0

C. 7

D. 9. Try multiplication.

E. 8

F. 9

Question 11

Be prepared to go slow – like 30 or 45 minutes or multiple days per problem. Do not help at all with these questions. When children comes across something new or unfamiliar, sometimes they have to learn things the hard way. The hard way is spending a lot of time thinking about a problem and trying different options. Once this approach becomes routine, this approach is no longer the hard way, it's the only way. If you are going to help with this problem, they are not going to learn the hard way because they have you to rely on instead of their own skills.

Make them show you how they solved the problem after each one – this solidifies learning and prevents them from guessing.

A. 0

B. 7; F = " × 4 ". You can ask your child to list the 4 arithmetic operators. If that doesn't work, ask them to try them all.

C. 10; "44 + 55" is a good starter problem for kids just learning double digit addition. A good way to help with this, if needed, is to start with "11 + 11", "11 + 12" , "11 + 23" and keep going until they get it. 33 + 77 is the next step.

D. 5

E. 3

F. 0

Question 12

Who would think that simple addition and subtraction (with the occasional multiplication throw in) would be so hard? If my children had to do these problems day after day, they would hate math. But for short periods of time, sporadically, surrounded by something more interesting, it works. The great thing about these problems is that picking up multiplication and division, factors, fractions, and exponents is really easy after this because the child is at a whole new thinking level.

A. 3

B. 12; (F = " × 2") Multiplication problems probably require a do over, and probably require the parent to ask "if addition doesn't work, can you try another operator? I use the term "operator" a lot in these questions.

    C. 8

    D. 20

    E. 5

    F. 0

Question 13

    A. 4

    B. 0

    C. 6 $F = \text{“} \times 3\text{”}$

    D. 27

    E. 9

    F. 6

Question 14

    A. 15

    B. 27

    C. 256 This is a super advanced SAT type skill in a simple format

    D. 0

    E. 0

    F. 4

Question 15

This level of difficulty is my end goal of second grade. It should be a challenge to get here. As a reminder, my goal is to overload working memory so that this is no longer a factor on any tests or academic skill for your child.   Next, I'm going to make each question take a long time so that your child learns and thinks as opposed to just calculates. Finally, I designed these questions so that your child will get them wrong at least once if not multiple times.   These are the 3 skills that make for a top academic performer. As a bonus, if you want a child who calculates arithmetic problems flawlessly, you will note that some of these problems require 8 or more arithmetic operations . It is reasonable for me to expect a child to perform arithmetic flawlessly after this type of work.

A. 10

B. 2

C. 15

D. 12; We don't go into negative numbers in this book, but you can explain this concept if your child doesn't grasp it yet. It's fun and exciting primarily because there is no reason for the child to know this concept. If your child is intrigued, put the book down and practice negative numbers. Interest in math is a more powerful teacher than workbooks in the long run.

E. 2

F. 6

You might also note that depending on where your child is currently in terms of skills, she might only accomplish one problem a day. If that is the case, hang in there, because you are on the right track.

Question 16

I think the best way to study for math of any type is word problems because word problems use a greater range of skills that are readily transferable to nonquantitative problems. The challenge for me as the home curriculum director is that there are other options like problems of this type, and if there is another option, we use it home. These problems are overkill for a cognitive skills test, but they have a big payoff for pre-algebra and algebra for obvious reasons. The one thing I won't do ever is practice math facts or do a math facts worksheet, even if one is assigned as homework; my child has to do it against my wishes.

A. 1

B. 3

C. 6

D. 16

E. 9

F. 8

Question 17

When a child shows a "gift" for math, and starts working ahead, a parent is tempted to provide them with workbooks featuring triple digit addition and subtraction, or multiplication and division. These are great concepts to think about but horrible and boring to practice. Math is about finding patterns and relationships, asking deep questions and discovery. Arithmetic worksheets do not teach or practice math. Worksheets practice calculation methods which are not part of math. The person who came up with the "Carry the 1" method was doing math. Those who use the method are not doing math but wasting a lot of time and learning to hate school.

Kids in grades 1 to 4 have to learn a bunch of skills to be good at math, which is the primary mission of this workbook. Doing lots of problems and arithmetic worksheets don't have to be part of the process.

A. 4

B. 8

C. 7

D. 9

E. 0

F. 4

These are really hard questions. Is it possible to make these questions even harder? Stay tuned for the next page of these problems.

Question 18

Just when you think we're going to practice something we learned, along comes another level of complexity. The cognitive skills tests aren't looking for "practiced" but instead are looking for "figure things out". Standardized test switched to this approach because the tests can be shorter and be a better predictor of school performance.

A. 0

B. 20

C. 28

D. 0

E. 15

F. 9

When I used to take arithmetic tests with pick lists, I could almost always guess or narrow the response down based on the answer clues. In this workbook, the answer clues point in the wrong direction half of the time. Guessing and the process of elimination play a vital but really tiny roll in cognitive skills tests. These two methods should not be used on every question, and if your child has success with one method or another and then tries to apply it broadly, break the bad habit.

Question 19

The bar was raised again.

I'm 96% sure that my questions are way harder than any questions in the quantitative section of the gifted and talented test. If your child takes a GAT test after doing this workbook, I will be emotionally devastated if they miss any question in the quantitative section. Standardized tests are even easier and school work is the easiest of all. If my son ever misses a question on a test a school, officially, I don't care in the slightest, but then I have to go cry in the closet.

    A. 2

    B. 13

    C. 1

    D. 0

    E. 22

    F. 6

Question 20

    A. 16

    B. 0

    C. 20

    D. 15 – No, there is no G in the 3rd equation

    E. 10

    F. The answer is 2. I can't believe that you and your child made it this far.

ABOUT THE AUTHOR

Brian Murray is an IT consultant, engineer, project manager and manager who lives in Chicago with his wife and two children who are both in the same GAT program. He was successful at math competition in high school, but did not develop a love of math until graduate school.

In 2011, after his first son was accepted to a GAT program, Brian became determined to get his second son into the same school. He bought a stack of test prep books and began reading academic papers on education, early childhood development, intelligence, cognitive skills, and anything written by test prep authors or their graduate students. While crafting a thousand super hard test questions, he realized that the tests were not measuring the child's ability to rotate a triangle or find a missing piece in a diagram, the tests were measuring thinking skills and problem solving skills.

Since his first child turned four, Brian has been home schooling math. He started to craft his own math problems based on the fundamentals of problem solving.

He has been writing a blog on how to get your slightly above average child into a GAT program since 2011.

You can follow his progress and his articles at www.getyourchildintogat.com.

Made in the USA
Middletown, DE
17 April 2017